get stupid!

Get Stupid!

WITH THE *IGNORANCE IS BLISS!* METHOD

T.O. STRONG

ARROGANT bookworms PUBLISHING ▪ TORONTO

Arrogant bookWorms Publishing
Toronto, Ontario, Canada

First edition, 2005
Copyright © 2005 Trevor Strong, all rights reserved.

Printed in Canada by Hignell Printing
Design, Typesetting & Illustration by Dana Samuel
    The headings are set in TheSans, designed by Luc(as) de Groot
    The text face is set in Minion, designed by Robert Slimbach

Library and Archives Canada Cataloguing in Publication

Strong, T. O. (Trevor O.), 1970–
    Get stupid! : with the Ignorance IS Bliss! method / T.O. Strong.
    ISBN 0-9736442-0-6
    1. Self-help techniques—Humor. 2. Success—Humor. I. Title.
    PN6231.S489S78 2004   C818'.602 C2004-905753-7

Acknowledgments

The Author would like to acknowledge all the idiots, twerps, and jackasses who have been trying to bring him down for years. Without the great conspiracy against him, the Author would never have been inspired to write this book. The Author would especially like to thank Mr. Morgan, his Grade 12 art teacher, for showing him how truly useless a person could be. I can see him now, gushing praise at all the little artist wannabes, his stupid ponytail dangling down the back of his cardigan. Well, Mr. Morgan, who ever got a job making charcoal drawings anyway? Let me tell you, mister, just because I didn't buy into your crap was no reason for you to give me an F. I knew what you were all about. I was doing fine making the moves on Missy Macmillan until you came along. All of a sudden she was talking about love and feelings, when all I wanted was a little action. I'm glad I went to the police and told them you were giving her "special lessons" after school. So what if I made it up. That's not the point. The point is that anyone who crosses me pays. You paid, that pizza guy who was five minutes late paid, my mother paid — oh yes, she paid dearly. If they'd stayed out of my way, they'd never have gotten hurt. But they were always in my face! So damn all of you. Damn you all to hell! I have no one to thank, no one to trust, and no one to believe in but myself.

Enjoy the book,

T.O. Strong

About the Author

T.O. Strong is a great, great man. Despite the conspiracy to destroy him, he has become the world's foremost expert on absolutely everything. He has dozens of degrees — an incredible feat, as he has never attended college — and has appeared at numerous television and radio stations demanding to be heard, only to be denied by the forces of darkness that control all media. Despite what she says, he does not have a wife, Beatrice, or two children, Lisa and T.O. Jr.

Mr. Strong lives somewhere but cannot be more specific out of fear for his personal safety.

He is not forty-nine years old.

Table of Contents

Introduction

ADMITTING YOU HAVE A PROBLEM
IS THE PROBLEM

We live in an almost perfect world. Food is abundant, we have comfortable shelter, and sex is available at a reasonable price. Yet most people are miserable.

Why this unhappiness? Is it a result of living in a hollow, materialistic society that places more value on transient goods than on the affairs of the soul? Of course not. The problem is much deeper than that.

Think of a cow. Is a cow happy? Well, yes it is. There it is chewing its cud, standing in a field — poo coming out of its bum — and it is fully and truly content. It doesn't know why it's there or what's going to happen next, and that's why it's happy. Now imagine that that cow *did* know what was going on. Do you think it'd be happy knowing it was about to be chopped up into a thousand little pieces? Probably not. Yet we've been led to believe that happiness lies in knowing the truth, when the reality is just the opposite.

What's Going On?
A famous dead French guy once said, "I think therefore I am."

Does this mean thinking is good? No. Let's revisit the statement:

I think therefore I am.

This statement is an equation. "I think" = "I am." Like any equation, it remains valid as long as what we apply to one side, we also apply to the other. So, add the word "not" to this and we get: "I think not" = "I am not." Or, in simple English:

I don't think therefore I aren't.

Now we're getting somewhere. Let's take it one step further. Let's add the word "it" to both sides, creating "I think it not" = "I am it not." Meaning:

I don't think about it therefore it isn't me!

This is the key to eternal happiness! If you don't think about something, then it doesn't apply to you. It simply goes away! All other self-help books are flawed because they conveniently miss this point. They tell you that admitting you have a problem is part of the solution, but in reality admitting you have a problem *is* the problem. It is only with the power of ignorance that bliss can be achieved. It is only once you *Get Stupid!* that you get happy.

Why This Book?

Why, indeed? With the number of self-help books currently on the market, you'd think there wouldn't be room for one more: *How to Cry Like a Man, What's Wrong With My Head?, How to Dress Your Inner Child, It's All Mommy's Fault* — how could any book improve on them? It's easy. They're the problem. This book is the solution.

Self-help books are bile-spewing garbage written to profit from your pitifulness. They're like my childhood dentist. After my checkup he'd give me a lollipop. Do you know why? So that my teeth would rot and he'd get more work. You see, writers of self-help books don't want you to get better, they want you to get worse. If self-help books actually worked, the people who wrote them would be out of jobs. And if the people who wrote them were all out of jobs, then the world economy would spiral into depression. You know why? Because *they* own everything.

Look at the facts. Farms can feed thousands and robots have replaced humans in the manufacture of goods. Therefore we shouldn't have to work! We should all be sitting on our butts eating cheesies on a tray brought by some cute little robot. But we aren't, are we? No, we're working harder than ever. Why? So we can afford the services of parasitic professions (like therapists, psychologists, teachers, and greeting-card writers) that waste time and money, and destroy our bliss. Why do we do this? Because they control us, that's why.

The brainwashing starts the moment you're born. You're told that thinking and feeling are good. But they are not! They are an evil cancer that eats at you from the inside until one day you find yourself wondering, "What is the meaning of my life?" You buy a self-help book to find the answer. It tells you that instead of being a little down, you actually have a poisoned childhood, an inner child with colic, and a former life that ended tragically when you were crushed after trying to prop up the last menhir at Stonehenge. You buy another book to solve this problem, which leads to another and another, until you're a complete basket case living in a basement stuffed with five-step programs and *Oprah* magazines. You're so desperate, you see a therapist. Now they really have you! You spend the rest of your life paying someone to listen to how pathetic you are.

I will not let this happen to you! That is why I have locked myself in this small room to write this book. They want to stop me, but they won't! I will not let another precious mind succumb to their thought-ful, evil ways. You must break the cycle! Stop thinking and feeling! *Get Stupid!*

It's So Easy!

Get Stupid! with the Ignorance IS Bliss! Method is the last self-help book you will ever read. In fact, it is the last book you will ever read. Once you've read it you'll know everything you'll ever need to know, maybe even less! You'll be amazed at how much better you feel when you feel nothing at all!

Here's how it works. First, take the IQ (Ignorance Quotient) test. This will give you an indication of how ignorant you are. If you pass the test (a great feat considering the strength of the conspiracy), you may go directly to the second half of the book. If you fail, you need my help, and it's up *The Seven Steps to Bliss!* for you. This program destroys bad habits — like thinking and feeling — one at a time until your mind is returned to its natural, blissful state. Once this is accom-plished you can move on to *Simplifying the World!* where I cut through the conspiracy's web of lies, topic by topic. This section also includes inspirational sayings guaranteed to sap your ambition. I fin-ish the book with letters from my fans and a glossary that tells you the *real* meaning of words.

"But if it's that simple, then how come we're in the mess we're in today?"

Good question.

How'd We Get So Messed Up?

GETTING BACK TO STUPID

There once was a time when people were blissfully ignorant. Hard to believe, isn't it? So, what happened? Was it a gradual decay into thinking or did the dark cloud of knowledge descend all at once? And what caused the blight of therapy to ravage the land? To answer these questions, I will now describe all of human history.

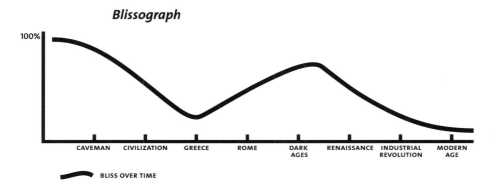

Blissograph

1. PREHISTORIC MAN

The Golden Age of Ignorance
In the beginning, people knew nothing and cared even less. Humanity had just left the trees and the novelty of walking was enough to get us through the day. This was the golden age of ignorance, when you could live your entire life without thinking. Cavemen didn't talk about "feelings of inadequacy" after a poor hunt or of a "need for self-fulfillment" after sitting in a cave for ten days hiding from lions. No. They ate. They reproduced. They were happy.

What made life so good back then was the wonderful lack of options. No one had to think, because there was nothing to think about. Stone Age job fairs consisted of only two booths, one labelled "Hunting" and the other "Gathering." The men went to the first booth and the women to the second. It was like this for tens of thousands of years. Then a third booth was set up. It was labelled "Farming." Ignorance would never be the same.

2. THE BIRTH OF CIVILIZATION

The Party Ends

One day, some cavepeople discovered that instead of gathering food, they could grow stuff in one place and save themselves a whole bunch of walking. This was the birth of farming. It was innocent enough at first, but soon the farmers grew more food than they could eat and a new occupation known as "the nobility" was born. Their duties were simple: they ate the farmers' food and in return bossed them around. This is called "civilization." How did they get away with this? With the creation of another fiendish invention: religion.

The nobility told the farmers about these powerful, magical beings called gods who would beat them up if they were not appeased. The only way to appease these gods was by giving them all your stuff. Unfortunately, only the nobility knew where these gods lived. So the farmers gave their stuff to the nobility, who promised to give it to the gods as soon as possible, but since the gods didn't actually exist, they just kept it for themselves.

The worst side-effect of religion was not poverty, however, but thought. People had decisions to make. "Should I sacrifice a lamb to Mu-Mu the Monkeyhead to ensure good crops," one would ponder, "or to Blumpt the Cosmic Slug so that my goats will bleat less loudly in the night?"

Things were getting messy, but this was just the start. Soon a civilization would be born with sillier notions than any that had come before it.

3. THE GREEKS

From Bad to Worse

The Greeks were an odd people who wrestled naked. They also had a great number of slaves, leaving them with very little to do. So little, in fact, that they invented philosophy to pass the time. Philosophy is the act of creating a silly theory and arguing about it with someone else who also has a silly theory. A favourite Greek debate centred on the "real" and the "ideal." They'd talk about what was real, and what was ideal, and what was ideally real, and how the real ideal would ideally deal with an ideal real, and whether the real ideal was ideally real or if it was really just an ideal real deal. All this talking made them so confused they barely noticed when they were conquered by the Romans.

4. THE ROMANS

Thinking Takes a Holiday

The Romans were a marked improvement over the Greeks. A generally ignorant people, most Romans gave little thought to the meaning of life and delighted in simple pleasures like eating until they threw up, drinking until they threw up, and watching lions eat people and then throw up. Sure, some dabbled in philosophy, but most were far too busy watching gladiators or beating their slaves to care. Unfortunately, this glorious resurgence of ignorance did not last long. The Emperor became converted to "Christianity," a new religion that not only made people give up their stuff, but also made them feel like they'd done something wrong. "Guilt" and "sin" replaced the violent pleasures of yesteryear, and the empire collapsed due to a lack of fun.

5. THE DARK AGES

Ignorance II — The Return

Out of the ruins of the Roman Empire came very little. Civilization and all the thinking that came with it were lost. The glorious Dark Ages had arrived. People worked, ate, slept, and died — not necessarily in that order. No one could read, and personal hygiene existed only in myth. Most people didn't even have pants. A blanket of stupidity covered the land like warm tar. It seemed mankind would never think again. It was too good to be true.

6. THE RENAISSANCE

The Revenge of the Greeks

Then a bunch of busybodies dug up all the stupid philosophies of the Greeks and started spreading them around. Some even began to read! A great deal of thinking was taking place, wasting time and making people miserable.

7. THE ENLIGHTENMENT

The Infection Spreads

The misguided learning of the Renaissance accelerated until people were no longer content with Greek hand-me-downs and started making up stupid theories of their own. Clumps of annoying, self-appointed experts appeared in salons, nattering on about absolutely everything. It became fashionable to be educated, reading was considered a virtue, and once beautifully empty minds were filling with unblissful thoughts at a frightening pace. The world was perilously close to the invention of therapy. Soon it would be too late.

8. THE INDUSTRIAL REVOLUTION

The Coming of the Dark Prince Freud

The Enlightenment paved the way for the Industrial Revolution. Machines began to replace human workers, leaving many people with nothing to do. Those who did nothing and did not get paid became the "homeless" and the "poor." Those who did nothing and got paid became the "middle class." Because the middle class lacked problems, they became very bored. So bored that they invented problems to get some attention. But no one listened to them. No one, that is, except Sigmund Freud.

Sigmund believed every boy wanted to have sex with his mother and toilet training was the most important stage of your life. It is incredible that a man so obviously insane would be allowed to judge others' mental health, but with his invention of "therapy" he was. His "therapy" was quite simple: the patient would lie down and complain, and Freud would pretend to listen. When the session ended, Freud would mention something about an "unresolved oral fixation," take the patient's money, and see him again every week for the rest of his life.

Freud's "therapy" was so successful that soon knock-offs flooded the market. Everyone wanted to get in on the action. Even people who didn't feel bad began feeling bad, simply because they didn't feel bad! They knew there must be something wrong with them if they didn't think there was something wrong with them! Not surprisingly, the therapists found something wrong with everyone. Even a rainy day would lead them to ask, "Are you down because of the weather, or are you suppressing a latent desire to resolve an Oedipal complex complicated by your anal expulsive behaviour?"

9. THE MODERN AGE

Self-help Is No Help at All

So far only the rich were infected with therapy, but soon the entire world became sick. The self-help book had arrived. These books contained all the ridiculous theories formerly reserved for the wealthy, in a cheap, convenient form. The lower classes, desperately wanting to be as emotionally damaged as the rich, rushed out to buy them. Inspired by their success, a cartel of therapists, self-help authors, and psychologists joined together to take over the world!

This was the great turning point. Before this moment, the destruction of bliss had been haphazard and unfocused. Now it was tightly controlled. The cartel grabbed all the levers of power. They forced children to attend schools where they were brainwashed. They made parents feel so inadequate that they bought books on "child-rearing" — something monkeys and penguins do with no books at all. Human life, once so full of absolutely nothing, became a crowded, thinking, feeling hell. The conspiracy's tentacles spread, yet still some ignorance lay untouched.

Then tragedy struck. The wholesome medium of television, the last sanctuary of stupidity, became corrupted by the self-help cabal. Where once there was Mr. Ed the talking horse and the hilarious antics of the Munsters, there was now Donahue. Oh, he looked innocent enough, with his grey hair and his habit of bouncing off into the audience, but he talked about feelings, and thoughts, and doubts, and closure. He twisted a nation of couch potatoes, forcing them to find "meaning" in their pathetic lives.

He was evil, but he was not the great Satan of self-help, just its herald. He was only paving the way for the coming of their leader — Oprah, the enthraller of masses. Her show was the final assault, a daily program encouraging everyone across the land to mope and weep and feel damaged. Everyone, everywhere, became so concerned with their "spirit" that they were unable to do anything but buy self-help books and Oprah magazines, and, in the end, submit to endless therapy. They had succeeded. All the money of the world now flowed to this nefarious group of self-help kingpins.

10. THE FUTURE

The Ignorant Shall Inherit the Earth

Yet one man remains!

I have escaped from their clutches! And by reading *Get Stupid! with the Ignorance IS Bliss Method* you will too! It is time to never think or care again! To return to the Stone Age, when men were men, women were women, and the only time you felt that gnawing feeling in your stomach was when you were actually being eaten!

Do not let them destroy you! Do not let them make you think you are a complicated person who needs nurturing! You are not! You are a primitive beast that would be perfectly happy if everyone would just leave you alone to gnaw on some bones!

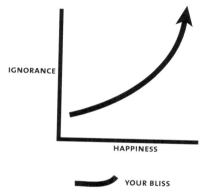

Join me on the crusade to end thought! End this pestilence of self-awareness! Put a Closed sign on your forehead! Deny the self-help conspiracy of another victim! And shout with me!

Get Stupid!
Get Stupid!
Stupid Get!

THE **ignorance quotient** TEST

The Ignorance Quotient Test

HOW LITTLE DO YOU KNOW?

The Ignorance Quotient Test provides an exact measure of your brain's blissfulness. Unfortunately, it is a rare person who manages to maintain ignorance in this horribly thoughtful world of ours. Only three people have passed this test on the first try — two were sportscasters and the third was in a coma. If you do pass, kudos to you! You don't need my help and can go directly to Part Two: *Simplifying the World!* If you fail — and don't worry, almost everyone does — then it's up *The Seven Steps to Bliss!* for you! Once you climb these stairs, you'll pass the test easily.

To grade your test, turn to page 102.

Good luck!

IGNORANCE QUOTIENT TEST

Questions

1. You are asked to point to Brazil on a map. You:
a) Point to Brazil.
b) Point to Swaziland.
c) Fall asleep.
d) Eat a sandwich.

2. A small child asks you how babies are made. You respond:
a) It all starts when the sperm of the male penetrates the egg of the female.
b) The stork brings them.
c) None of your damn business.
d) I don't know, I don't work in a factory.

3. You've just won $10 million in the lottery. You:
a) Pay off all outstanding debts, buy a reasonable house, and invest the rest for your future.
b) Buy a fast car and a trophy spouse.
c) Lose the ticket.
d) Drink yourself to death.

4. If a tree falls in the forest and no one is around to hear it, does it make a sound?
a) Without someone to perceive it, the sound does not truly exist.
b) Yes, it makes a sound.
c) It screams, "Help, I'm falling! Why can't anyone hear me?"
d) Huh?

5. When you have a sharp pain in your mouth, you:
a) Go to the dentist.
b) Hope it goes away.
c) Drink until you feel better.
d) Get out the pliers and pull out teeth until you find the one that hurts.

6. Your boss is coming over for dinner. You:
a) Prepare a fine meal.
b) Get your spouse to prepare a fine meal.
c) Tell your boss to make dinner.
d) Drug your boss and steal his wallet.

7. You're trapped on a desert island with only one item. You bring:
a) A radio-transmitter to call for help.
b) A Swiss army knife.
c) The special anniversary edition of *Hustler*.
d) An electric can opener.

8. Do you work to live or live to work?
a) Work to live.
b) Live to work.
c) Walk to work.
d) Live in a wok.

9. You are in a crowded theatre watching a movie. You smell something burning. You:
a) Yell "Fire!" and run for the exit.
b) Run for the exit, so you'll be the first one out, and then yell "Fire!"
c) Yell "Fire!" and let everyone else out first, then search the floor for dropped wallets and purses.
d) Do nothing, it's only a movie.

10. Your spouse is deathly ill. You have no money and cannot afford to buy the medicine at the drugstore to save him/her. You:

a) Do whatever you can to make the money you need to buy the medicine.

b) Break into the drugstore and steal the medicine.

c) Tell your spouse to get a job.

d) Sell your spouse to slave traders and buy a new home-entertainment system.

11. Do you exercise regularly?

a) Yes.

b) No.

c) I exercise my right to bear arms.

d) I like fudge.

12. Fourteen monkeys magically appear in your bathroom and start eating your toilet. Three olive-coloured laundry machines howl like cows and dance the mamba while your feet turn into pomegranates. You:

a) Wake up from your dream.

b) Wait for the drugs to wear off.

c) Eat a truckload of pink wombats.

d) Say, "Not again."

13. What is the "golden rule"?

a) Do unto others as you would have them do unto you.

b) Do unto others before they do unto you.

c) Do others.

d) Never leave beer unattended.

14. If you were granted one wish, what would you wish for?

a) World peace.

b) A million more wishes.

c) A lifelong supply of cheesies.

d) A funny midget dancing with a talking dog.

15. You find a wallet containing $500, a bunch of credit cards, and ID with the address of the owner. You:

a) Return the wallet anonymously.

b) Return the wallet and repeatedly mention how lucky this person was that you found it and not someone else, until he finally gives you a reward.

c) Take the money and leave the wallet.

d) Impersonate the person and go on a spending spree, then get caught at a bar in Tijuana bragging about it to your new friend, Sanchez.

16. React to the following statement: "It is better to give than to receive."

a) True.

b) False.

c) Only in the case of sexually transmitted diseases.

d) Brazil.

17. The pyramids were made by:

a) The ancient Egyptians.

b) Putting a bunch of stones on top of each other.

c) Aliens.

d) Me. With some help from my buddy Charlie, who's drunk most of the time so he really wasn't all that much help at all, but we got it done.

18. The doctor tells you that you have only one day left to live. What do you do?

a) Spend the day with family and loved ones and gather one last time to watch the sun set.

b) Get a second opinion.

c) Watch television, eat a pizza, and call in a prostitute.

d) Have a nap.

19. You wake up in the middle of the night with a miraculous vision of the dawning of a new day. You:

a) Write down your thoughts and spread the word to a waiting world.

b) Go back to sleep. You'll remember it in the morning if it's really important.

c) Make yourself a sandwich.

d) Stay up until you see the dawning of a new day, then go to sleep.

20. To be or not to be? That is the question. The answer is:

a) There is no real answer; it is merely an expression of angst.

b) To be.

c) Not to be.

d) Swaziland.

21. True or false?
a) True.
b) False.
c) Tralse.
d) Frue.

22. The reason we do not float off into space is that we are pulled towards the earth by:
a) Gravity.
b) Heaviness.
c) Our shoes.
d) Tiny invisible elves.

23. If you don't have anything good to say, it's best to:
a) Not say anything at all.
b) Say it.
c) Scream it out at the top of your lungs.
d) Fight.

24. React to this statement: "A mind is a terrible thing to waste."
a) True, you should always maximize your mental potential.
b) True, everyone should be given equal access to education.
c) True, like the Native Americans we should use 100 per cent of the buffalo.
d) False. I'm wasted and I feel fine.

25. You are at a bar and someone "accidentally" bumps into you. You:
a) Say, "Excuse me."
b) Say, "Watch where you're going, buddy!"
c) Smash a bottle over the offender's head.
d) Throw up and pass out in your own vomit.

part one

THE SEVEN STEPS TO BLISS!

The Seven Steps to Bliss!

DOWNSIZE YOUR MIND!

You failed the Ignorance Quotient Test, but do not despair. You may know something now, but soon you won't know anything. You see, your mind is a suitcase stuffed with heavy and unnecessary items like thoughts, emotions, skills, aspirations, and dreams. This baggage weighs you down, making it hard to check in on the airplane of life. It's time to pack light! Throw out that luggage and board that plane with nothing more that a small carry-on bag called ignorance.

"But how can I do this?" you ask. It's easy — just climb up *The Seven Steps to Bliss!* By the time you get to the top, your head will be as empty as a public school with an asbestos scare. Don't worry, you will still have a wonderful mental life full of arguments and opinions, but now what you say will be ill-informed and arbitrary. You will never again experience that annoying feeling of changing your mind.

The incredible pressure of *The Seven Steps to Bliss!* program will turn your mushy swamp of a brain into a nice hard lump of coal. You think the moon is made of linguini? Then it is. And no one will ever be able to convince you otherwise — not the therapists, not the scientists, not even those pesky astronauts. You will become totally immune to the poisonous thinking around you.

"But how do I get to this blissful state?" you may ask. "It seems so hard." But it isn't. It's easy. So come with me and let's make our way up *The Seven Steps to Bliss!*

The Seven Steps to Bliss!
1. *Stop thinking!* — empty your brain!
2. *Shift the Blame!* — blame others!
3. *Lose Touch with Your Feelings!* — delete your emotions!
4. *Build Walls!* — keep out everything but you!
5. *Avoid Challenges!* — never fail by never trying to succeed!
6. *Believe in Yourself!* — love you and only you!
7. *Deny, Deny, Deny!* — your truth is the only truth!

I bet you feel better already. So get rid of those bad habits, thoughts, and feelings, and let's *Get Stupid!*

STEP ONE — STOP THINKING!

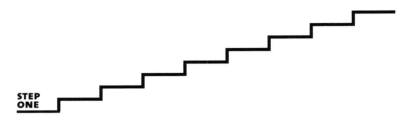

**STEP
ONE**

A Mind Is a Terrible Thing!

Ignorance IS Bliss! Think about this for a second (but no longer). If *Ignorance IS Bliss!* — as "intelligent" people often say — then why aren't you ignorant? If ignorance is the road to true happiness, then why aren't you on it? Because the conspiracy has made you take another road, that's why! They've put you on a detour down Misery Lane where all the signs say, "Know Yourself!" Why? Because when you "know yourself" you discover just how pitiful, petty, and puny you really are. How everything you've ever done has been a failure, how your relationships are disasters, how it was your fault that your marriage fell apart when you know she was sleeping around!

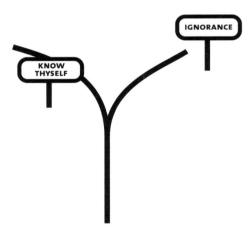

The conspiracy wants you to be a loser so that you'll be dependent on them. But how would you feel if, instead of thinking more about yourself, you actually thought *less*? What if, instead of dwelling on your faults and failures, you simply ignored them? You'd feel pretty good, wouldn't you? But how do you become ignorant? It's easy. Just *Stop Thinking!*

"But how do I do this?" The answer is, you probably already have. Have you ever said something without thinking first? Maybe you've made fun of someone just because they looked different? That's ignorant. Perhaps you've gone to another country and thought, "Why don't they learn to speak English?" That shows a definite lack of thought. Have you ever turned on the news to see pictures of yet another famine in some godforsaken country and said, "Get a job!" Now, that's stupid! Good work!

Ignorance is an aggressive apathy towards everything except your personal well-being. It's the ability to use 10 per cent of 10 per cent of 10 per cent of your brain, just like a turnip. Take a moment now and *Stop Thinking!*

Felt good, didn't it? But this is just the beginning. The real challenge is to *Stop Thinking!* in the outside world. Take newspapers, for example. What do you read? If you've been reading stories about "politics" or "foreign affairs," stop. These things are of no concern to you. So what if there's a slaughter in Crapatania? You don't live there and they shouldn't burden you with their problems. You're not the one killing women and children! You don't call *them* up when you're in the bathroom and realize there's no toilet paper. No, that would be rude. So, if you read a newspaper, just open it to sports and mumble about what you would do if you were the coach. Then flip to the cartoons. Read only the simple ones — no *Doonesbury.* Then throw it on the floor. Soon you'll ignore newspapers altogether and lose the ability to read. Just like that, you're miles down the road to ignorance!

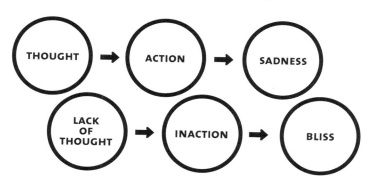

So far so good, but it's easy to *Stop Thinking!* about new things. What about the stuff you already know? How do you *Stop Thinking!* about that?

It is a well-known fact that the human mind is only so big and that there is a limit to what it can hold. When we are younger, our brains

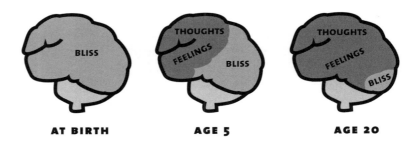

| AT BIRTH | AGE 5 | AGE 20 |

are not empty, as is commonly thought, but full of bliss. But when we learn, the bliss is forced out by knowledge, and by the time we're adults, it's all gone. But you *can* get the bliss back in! How? By filling your mind with blissful, ignorant things!

A good start is television. Quality programs like *Entertainment Tonight* and *Jerry Springer* will assault your knowledge with such force that it will cascade out your ears and writhe upon the floor, where it will beg you to put it out of its misery. You can also focus on your basic needs. Spend an entire day wondering where you should scratch yourself. Take a week debating which finger is best to pick your nose with. Set aside a month to sit and eat cheese. Thoughts will spurt from your eyes!

But be warned. People will try to stop you! They will not understand why you've decided to *Stop Thinking!* They have been brainwashed! They believe that thinking is good! They'll want to talk to you and explain things. Don't let them! If someone comes towards you, jump in the bushes. If they spot you, let out a hissing sound, curl your hand into a claw, and swipe at them. This usually works. If you cannot escape conversation, just nod your head and dream about what kind of sandwich you want for lunch. Don't listen!

Exciting things happen when you *Stop Thinking!* You not only lose knowledge, but also car keys, relationships, and possibly your job. Don't feel bad about this. Every time you lose something, another dangerous source of knowledge is eliminated. No more driving! No more deadlines! You can focus on the important things in life — like scratching yourself. Ah, the bliss!

Well, enough of Step One, there's so much more to show you! Do your exercises and join me in the next chapter.

Remember!

1. Don't think!
2. Watch television until your eyes bleed, then watch it some more.
3. Answer all questions with "Shut up."
4. Eat with your hands. Except for finger foods, which you should eat directly with your mouth.
5. Bathe just enough to avoid the habitation of your body by rodent-sized animals.
6. You may not be able to control the world, but you sure can ignore it.

Exercises

1. Find someone in need and offer suggestions on self-improvement with total disregard for his or her circumstances. For example, tell a homeless person to "Buy a house!"
2. Park in a handicapped spot. If a handicapped person is occupying the spot, yell, "You gimps get so many perks that I'm thinking of cutting my own leg off!"
3. Go to a local school at recess and smoke in front of the children. If a teacher confronts you, yell at him, using as much profanity as possible.
4. Keep a journal to chart your progress as you stop thinking. Forget where you put it.
5. Watch *Jeopardy* on television and try to answer the questions. Punch yourself in the face each time you get one right.

STEP TWO — SHIFT THE BLAME!

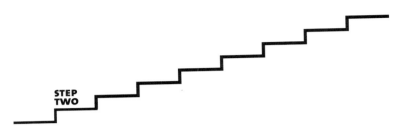

STEP
TWO

Fingers Are for Pointing!

Have you managed to *Stop Thinking!*? You're not sure? Great! You've made real progress, but there's a lot of work ahead. You see, sometimes you *Stop Thinking!* but the problem does not go away. In these situations you must take action! You must *Shift the Blame!*

Let's start with an example. You're watching the news and see a story on drunk driving and its effects. How do you respond? If you've managed to *Stop Thinking!* you'll say, "Who cares?" and make jokes at the expense of the victims. Pretty easy. Now, let's make it harder. Let's say that you *are* "drunk driving and its effects." You've had fourteen daiquiris and smash your car into a telephone pole. You *Stop Thinking!* but it's not enough. Your car is wrecked and the police are coming. It looks like you'll have to admit you did something wrong, leading to guilty feelings and the purchase of a new self-help book, right? Wrong. It's merely time to *Shift the Blame!*

It's easy!

You're not at fault. Others *are* responsible for your car's surprise parking job. How does this work? Just find someone — anyone — and point the finger of blame at them. The bar that made you drink is the most obvious place to start. How can they sell alcohol to someone as irresponsible as you?

But what if you were drinking at home? No problem. There are lots of people to blame. How about the telephone company? Why did they put those poles so close to the road? Negligence! They should know better! They could kill somebody, especially with those bars getting people drunk and forcing them to drive.

And then there's the car company. They shouldn't make cars that drunk people can drive. Don't they know that's dangerous? In fact, they shouldn't be making cars at all! Just look at all the accidents they're causing!

And the police? They treated you like a common criminal when the accident wasn't even your fault. What abuse! What mistreatment! What a miscarriage of justice!

And what about your mother? What kind of mom would raise a child who would be so easily duped by bar staff, telephone companies, car makers, and police officers? A mother who is to blame! A mother who always wished you were a daughter! A mother who dressed you up in skirts and called you Betty. A mother who never loved me!

And what about God? If God created the world, and is everything and everywhere, then there must be a divine purpose to your accident. God made you hit that pole as part of His divine plan. God made booze! God made cars! God made your mother! It's not your fault. God did it!

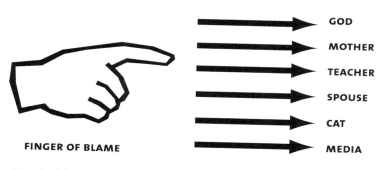

GOD

MOTHER

TEACHER

SPOUSE

CAT

FINGER OF BLAME   MEDIA

Get the idea? When you *Shift the Blame!* you can do anything you want without ever worrying about the consequences. You can't be wrong when you don't know what's right! And if you didn't do it, then someone else did. It's that simple.

But *Shift the Blame!* is not a technique confined to the here and now. You can also *Shift the Blame!* for things that have already happened. Are you feeling guilty because that fat kid you teased in high school had a mental breakdown? Don't be, just *Shift the Blame!* His breakdown wasn't your fault. It was his parents' fault! They should never have let the little porker go to school, all pudgy and wobbly, with his distended stomach spilling out the bottom of his shirt like beige Jell-O. How could you possibly resist yelling "Fatty fatty two-by-four, couldn't get through the bathroom door" when the little chubster's pants split open while he was giving a speech on ear lice? He never should have been sent to school in the first place! The school's to blame as well! They should have put thunder-thighs in a special class with all the other ugly, oddball children so that the normal kids wouldn't be forced to see him every day. How can anybody be expected to resist mocking someone so odd and unpopular? It wasn't your fault at all! It was the school's! And God's! And your mother's!

Please take a moment now to *Shift the Blame!* for all those things you've been feeling guilty about.

Done? Good. Now let's focus on your relationships. Has your marriage failed? Don't feel bad, just *Shift the Blame!* Sure, your spouse found you in bed with half the staff from Arby's — but that's Arby's fault. They should never have hired such easy, nubile workers! And the bed manufacturers are guilty too. Why did they make such a durable bed? And the government! They made roads! Roads that lead to Arby's! And your wife. Why didn't she call before coming back from the gym early? Didn't she think I might be busy? That maybe I had my own life? And we all know what she was up to at the "gym" anyway, don't we? She drove me into the arms of the night shift! IT WAS ALL HER FAULT! And my mother's too. Oh, and God's.

See how easy it is? Now it's time for you to put *Shift the Blame!* into action!

Remember!

1. It's someone else's fault.
2. Forgive yourself without exception — others have a lot to answer for.
3. Lies, told well, are a blessing.
4. There is nothing in the world you can't pin on someone else.

Exercises

1. Go outside and kick the neighbours' cat. Blame someone else.
2. If you have a job, stop working. If they fire you, write a letter blaming others. Send it to as many boards and tribunals as you can. You will be astounded by the reaction and may even get your job back.
3. Call up your parents and blame them for everything that has ever gone wrong with your life. If they say, "You need to take a little responsibility," tell them to stop turning it around on you. Then say, "I wish I were an orphan. That way you'd be dead!"
4. Make a list of all the bad habits you would like to rid yourself of. Don't try to quit, just *Shift the Blame!* For example:

Bad Habit	Blame
Eating Pop-Tarts	Advertising
Bad temper	Television
Public urination	The Devil
Obsessive compulsions	Martha Stewart

5. Stop paying your bills. When companies call to collect, tell them it's their fault you're not paying. Tell the utility company that their electricity wasn't good, the cable company that there was nothing to watch on TV, and the phone company that you didn't have one good conversation all month.

STEP THREE — LOSE TOUCH WITH YOUR FEELINGS!

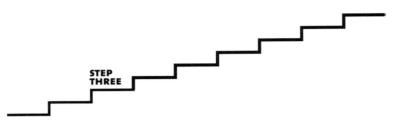

STEP
THREE

Smother Your Inner Child!

Now that you have learned to *Stop Thinking!* and *Shift the Blame!* it's time we talk about feelings. "Oh," you say, "I knew this was going to happen — all the other books talk about feelings too. They talk about how important feelings are, how they should be brought out, and how they heal." Once again, you have been deceived. Feelings are not good. No, they are very, very bad. They are unnatural urges planted by therapists and greeting-card companies to leave you weak and dependent. Instead of getting in touch with your feelings, you should *Lose Touch With Your Feelings!*

This is harder than it sounds, for feelings have been forced into you since you were a child. First *Sesame Street* made you "feel" with its furry, footless monsters. Then, as you grew older, more feelings were added by schools, parents, and Disney movies. Soon some of these emotions became tangled up in big messy bundles. These bundles are called "complexes" and are very dangerous. They come in many forms, but perhaps the most common is the "inner child," a younger version of yourself that often forms in the bowels. How do you know if you have one?

Here are the symptoms:

Inner Child Symptoms
occasional bouts of wild-eyed wonder
distended stomach
urge to suck your thumb
excessive gas

If you have an inner child, what then? The therapists will tell you to give birth to it. Don't! Once it's out it will only remind you of how

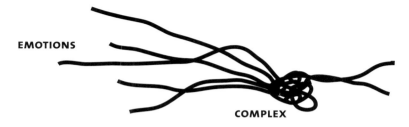

EMOTIONS

COMPLEX

much fun you had as a child, when all you did was eat ice cream and make fun of that fat kid. And you'll compare this to how you are today — poor, busting your ass, surrounded by ungrateful, selfish people — and you will cry.

But what if your inner child is already out? Then you must kill it. How? Take it by its slimy little hand and drag it around with you. Make it do your lousy job, talk to your lousy relatives, attend your lousy court hearings, and live your lousy life. Soon it will take up smoking, hang out in strip joints, throw pennies at the dancers, drink a quart of vodka, swallow a jar of pills, pass out in its little crib, and choke on its own vomit.

Ah… now that your inner child is sleeping in its tiny grave, it's time to tackle the next complex — the masculine/feminine side. This is the growth of a member of the opposite sex on one of your shoulders. Therapists, of course, encourage you to grow it even bigger, saying, "It's the most natural thing in the world." But it's not. Men are men and women are women. Dogs don't have a "cat" side, pumpkins don't have a "turnip" side, and chainsaws don't have a "lathe" side. Get rid of it quickly or soon you won't be able to walk, especially if you're still carrying around that inner child. Here are the symptoms:

Symptoms of a Male Having a Female Side
believes there are two sides to every argument
places the toilet seat down
cries during touching commercials
grows breasts

Symptoms of a Female Having a Male Side
prefers hockey to figure skating
random public belching and scratching
loses interest in shoes
increased armpit odour

If you have these symptoms, you must act quickly. If you are a man with a feminine side, go to a strip club, grab a seat beside someone's inner child, and get drunk. That should snap you back. If you are a woman with a masculine side, then you too should go to a strip club and get drunk. Once you've seen how low and disgusting men are, you will not dare let this side near you again.

Now that you've untangled your complexes, it's time to *Lose Touch With Your Feelings!* one at a time. How? By ignoring them. Remember: *Ignorance IS Bliss!* Feelings, you see, are like annoying friends. If you continue to return their phone calls and send them Christmas cards, they will drop by to visit at the most inopportune times. But if you rip the phone out of the wall and burn all your mail, you'll soon lose touch and they'll just have to find someone else to bother.

But be warned, feelings are persistent. They will do whatever they can to stick to you. You must be strong and ignore them completely. Don't cry at weddings. Don't laugh at jokes. Don't feel bad when your father abandons you, leaving you alone with your drunk, crazy mother. Don't worry that maybe this is a pattern you are repeating with your own children.... DON'T CARE! When you don't care, love vanishes (you can't love someone you don't care about), guilt disappears (you can't feel guilty when you don't care about what you did), and sorrow evaporates (you can't be sad when all you care about is you!). You will become a happy, hollow shell of your former self — as deep as a puddle and as wide as the sea!

Remember!
1. If you don't feel, you can't hurt.
2. Love is strong, but apathy is stronger.
3. Never be mistaken for someone who cares.
4. Crying is acceptable only if you are peeling an onion or have been pepper-sprayed.

Exercises
1. Walk by people less fortunate than you. Do not imagine what it would be like to live in their shoes.
2. Go to films with touching death scenes and when people cry, yell, "It's only a movie!"
3. At your next birthday party, open each present and say, "What is this crap?"

4. Make a list of all those people who are close to you. Talk to them one at a time and ask them if they love you. When they say, "Yes," answer, "I know the games you're playing!"
5. Wait for some feelings to come to you. When they arrive, bash your head against a wall. This will associate feelings with pain, causing you to have fewer feelings.

STEP FOUR — BUILD WALLS!

STEP FOUR

Become Emperor of Your Emotional Real Estate!

Now that your inner child is in its tiny grave, your masculine/feminine side has left you, and your feelings have been pushed far away, it's time for you to *Build Walls!* to make sure they never come back. Or, if they do come back, that they can't get in to see you.

"But I've just spent years tearing my walls *down*!" you say. Well, find those old bricks and make some mortar.

History teaches us that walls are good. You can't be strong without walls. Kings live in castles with walls, China has a big wall, and the largest retail company on earth is Wal-Mart. In fact, if you don't have a wall, you can bet your booties that someone who does is going to pay you a visit and beat the crap out of you. What have they got to lose? You can't hurt them. They have walls! They'll grind you into a pulp and all you'll do is cry because your unwanted feelings will have snuck back in.

You've probably been told that removing your walls is the first step to a happy life. Let me ask you a question. Would you live in a house with no walls? Of course not. But by eliminating your emotional barriers, this is just what you are doing. You're letting people move into your *Emotional Real Estate.* There is only so much room inside any home and, if you're not careful, you'll soon have a house full of unruly, freeloading boarders, eating your food, playing loud music, and having parties late into the night. They'll turn your house into a crack den, defecate in the corners, and use the curtains as toilet paper. Don't let this happen to you! *Build Walls!* now!

This is a good time to remind yourself why you built walls in the first place. Did someone hurt you? Of course they did, and you very logically built a wall so it wouldn't happen again. Why would you tear it down now? They'll destroy you! No, you should be building bigger, better walls to ensure your emotional security! But don't stop with the walls. Install a psychological burglar alarm to warn you of intruders.

Train a mental pit bull to tear trespassers apart. Stock up on ten years of psychic canned goods to survive any siege!

Who are these people squatting on your *Emotional Real Estate*, anyway? Probably "friends" and "family" who want to make you feel bad about leaving them out in the cold. But why are they cold? They are cold because their *Emotional Real Estate* has no walls. Of course they want to get into your nice, warm house. There they are, knocking at your door. Maybe they'll tell you their car has broken down and they just want to use the phone or that they're lonely and your children need you. Don't be fooled!

Remember, alienation is a good thing. It sets you apart. It allows you to be your own person and no one else's. It gives you the confidence to treat others the way they deserve to be treated: to tell the paperboy to go screw himself when he waves to you on the street. To tell your neighbour that it's "None of your goddamn business!" when she rudely asks, "How are you doing today?" To tell that lawyer to "Get off my lawn before I blow you to kingdom come" when he shows up with another set of fraudulent papers.

But emotional barriers can go only so far. Physical barriers are just as important. Get some bricks, board up the windows, and booby-trap the doors! Then buy a real alarm system, train a real pit bull, stock up on ten years of real canned goods, and never go outside

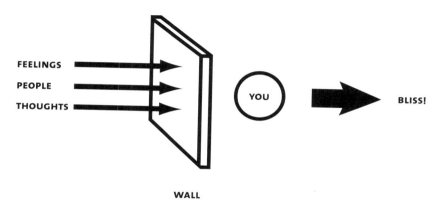

WALL

again. Don't open your door — not even for the pizza guy. He can leave it on the step. It's just you, your dog Attila, cheesies, and a satellite dish. When they come to get you, you'll be ready. And they will come. You can bet on it. I think I hear them now! I'm sure that's them. You won't get me! I know you want to stop me, but I will not be stopped, the truth will be told! I'm ready... come on... um... Oh, I guess it wasn't them after all.

Congratulations! Your home is now your castle, and you are truly *Emperor of your Emotional Real Estate!*

Remember!
1. Don't talk to anyone.
2. Home is where you rack your guns.
3. Make a shopping list of things you might need, like attack dogs, barbwire, firearms, knives, large threatening signs, baseball bats, and comic books.
4. Never let anyone in. Not even a vacuum cleaner salesman.
5. The only person who cares about you is you.
6. People who want to hug you are only trying to steal your life force.

Exercises
1. Make the place where you live as uninviting as possible. Leave broken glass on the front step and put your attack dogs on frayed ropes that are ready to break at any moment.
2. Invite some of your old friends over and ignore them. See how long it takes them to go away. If they are persistent, release the dogs.
3. Do not go outside for an entire day. Then double it. Keep on doubling it until you no longer go outside at all.
4. Write up a list of all the things people have done to wrong you over the years, and reasons why you are better off without them.
5. Create a personal manifesto to justify your hermit-like existence.

STEP FIVE — AVOID CHALLENGES!

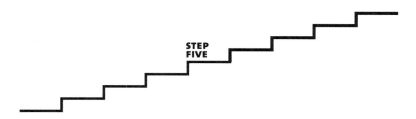

STEP
FIVE

Aim Low and You Will Never Be Disappointed!

You probably feel safe with the nice new walls you've built, but beware! There is still a danger that lives *inside* your walls — your inner voice! Your inner voice is the sirens' call luring you towards the beautiful shore of hope, and then dashing you against the rocks of failure. It tells you to "do your best" and that "anything is possible if you work hard enough." Do not listen! Plug your ears, turn away, and *Avoid Challenges!*

Yes, I know you've been told to challenge yourself, but challenges are bad. Have you ever read a "challenging" book? It sucked, didn't it? Not convinced? The space shuttle *Challenger* actually exploded. Do you want to explode?

Don't expect anything out of life. Set your sights low and you will never be disappointed. The worst that can happen is you'll get the smug satisfaction of being proved right. You see, depression is not caused by parents calling their children stupid, ugly, and fat. No, it's caused by parents calling their children smart, pretty, and slender when they actually *are* stupid, ugly, and fat. This condemns them to a lifetime of challenge as they try living up to their own self-image. If kids were told they were worthless in the first place, they could accept their mediocre lives. But no, they are told, "You can be anything you want to be." How cruel. Ugly Mary is never going to be a model. Drooling Martin won't be a movie star. And I am never going to be a superhero.

Yes, I too was told I could be anything. So I spent twenty years of my life hanging out at chemical dumps, sneaking into nuclear power plants, and climbing up bell towers during thunderstorms trying to trigger my latent supernatural powers, but nothing! I was in intensive care dozens of times for skin grafts, or to get a finger reattached, but the best I ever did was glow pale green for a week — then it passed and all my teeth fell out. It would have been a lousy power anyway. What was I going to call myself? Dimboy? Or the Human Indiglow? Maybe I could have helped somebody find her keys in the dark, but that was hardly going to get me membership in the Legion of Superheroes. I wasn't even bright enough to read by. So don't expect anything out of life. It just isn't going to happen.

Abandon your dreams! This is the best way to *Avoid Challenges!* Simply think of what you want to be and then convince yourself it's impossible. Do you want to be a doctor? Well, you can't. The training's too expensive, you're too stupid, and your name is already long enough without adding "Dr." to it. Or maybe you want to be a janitor — same thing. You can't afford the training, you're too stupid, and you'd always be drinking the cleaning fluid. Think of how happy you'll be by giving up! And how about all the time and money you'll save! Now you can focus on the important things like buying a kick-ass stereo to play your AC/DC box set on.

Now that you're rid of what you want to be, you must get rid of what you are. Do you still have a job? Is it difficult? Quit! Give your boss the finger and say goodbye to early mornings! Is your spouse getting on your case because you don't have any ambition, you just quit your job, and you spend all your time listening to AC/DC? You're better off by yourself! You're better off with nothing at all! Avoid everything! Because when you avoid everything, you have nothing left to deal with. And then life isn't a challenge, is it?

Remember!
1. You only fail when you try.
2. There are no obstacles in life that cannot be ignored.
3. No pain, no pain.
4. It's easier not to do the hardest thing than it is to do the easiest thing.
5. Life is a race. Be a spectator.
6. If at first you don't succeed, give up!

Exercises
1. Make a list of all your hopes and dreams and throw it in the fire.
2. Always be kind by telling others that they will fail.
3. If you have children, go to parent/teacher night. Inform the teacher that you are taking your children out of class because you've had enough of them coming home with all those fancy notions in their heads. You know the kids are going nowhere and no one should tell them otherwise!
4. If you find it a struggle to get out of bed in the morning, just don't bother. Another morning will come soon enough.
5. Make a list of people who challenged themselves and died, as a reminder that all their hard work was for nothing.

STEP SIX — BELIEVE IN YOURSELF!

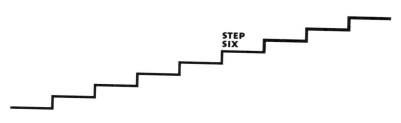

And No One Else!

You may have noticed over the course of this program that your life has already changed. By now you are living alone, seldom venturing out, and talking only to yourself. You have no goals or ambitions and spend most of your time staring at the wall. If you are not totally alone, please review the previous chapters and find where you went wrong. If you are alone, do not be lonely. You have the best company on earth — you!

It's time for you to *Believe in Yourself!* — and no one else.

Remember, it's a mystery why anyone but you was even put on earth. Other people have no purpose except to annoy you. You are the keeper of absolute truth and everyone else is an idiot. Sure, they'll disagree. You've probably already had to deal with your so-called "friends" trying to stop you from finishing this program. They might have said such things as "You've changed," "It's that book you're reading, isn't it?" and "For the love of God, call off your dogs!" Do not be persuaded. Tell them, "You don't know what the hell you're talking about!" If this fails, say, "Wait here while I go get my gun."

Now they're calling you "crazy" and "nuts." They are jealous. You have found true happiness while they are trapped in their world of thoughts and feelings. They are too weak to be ignorant. They still need family, jobs, and love, while you are beyond such things. You *Believe in Yourself!* You are perfect. They're the ones living challenging, disappointing lives! They're the crazy ones trying to bring you down, to deny you your right to ignorance! But you know better. You know that *Ignorance IS Bliss!*

So *Believe in Yourself!* as they sue you because your pit bull mauled them. *Believe in Yourself!* as the city fines you for not mowing your lawn for three months. *Believe in Yourself!* as the police pound on your door to charge you with fictitious crimes created by the therapists. Remember, they are wrong! You can do anything you want! They should be grateful that you even allow them to exist.

Have I told you about the people who have tried to bring me down? Of the endless parade of supposed ex-wives trying to get me to pay child support, just because they weren't careful? Of the credit-card companies with the nerve to say I owe them money? Well, if they wanted the money so badly, they shouldn't have given it to me in the first place. As far as I'm concerned, it was a present. And then there are those little old ladies who some lawyer whipped up into a frenzy that keep suing me. Look, they gave me that money, fair and square. I was perfectly within my rights to say I was collecting for the Red Cross. I never said which Red Cross I was collecting for. It was *my* Red Cross, okay?

But they will never get me! I am too great and too powerful! They are the goop that clings to the muck that clings to the gum that clings to the dirt that clings to the bottom of my shoe! They are so far beneath me that they dwell in the centre of the earth! They are so insignificant that a microscope could not detect their presence. I am so ignorant that I don't even know they exist! Yet still they come, trying to bring me down. Their pettiness and jealousy shall never win, because I am perfect! I am right! I believe in myself! I believe! And you who are reading this book, you who are on the second-last step, you too must *Believe in Yourself!* You are all that matters!

I must warn you, however, that it is hard being the only person in the world who is right. It is a terrible burden that you must use all your strength to ignore. You will be frustrated when you meet people who do not know that you are perfect. Some will even tell you that you're wrong. But you know the truth! They have been programmed by Oprah and Dr. Phil. They are thinking, feeling automatons! Only you are correct. Only you are glorious. There is only one centre and it is you. All others are mere satellites drawn towards your massive gravity and then incinerated in your atmosphere! *Believe!* The more convinced you are that you are right, the more obvious it becomes that everyone else is wrong. Oh, they will challenge you for a while, but stay firm. Soon they will leave you alone. People are willing to take only so many pit-bull attacks and gunshot wounds. And then there will be peace and silence. And you will be happy, living with the only person who deserves to be in your presence — you!

So get to work — you're almost done!

Remember!

1. You are right.
2. They are wrong.
3. You are right.
4. They are wrong.
5. You are right.
6. They are wrong.
7. You are right.
8. They are wrong.
9. You are right.
10. They are wrong.
11. You are right.
12. They are wrong.
13. You are right.
14. They are wrong.
15. You are right.
16. They are wrong.
17. You are right.
18. They are wrong.
19. You are right.
20. They are wrong.
21. You are right.
22. They are wrong.
23. You are right.
24. They are wrong.
25. You are right.
26. They are wrong.
27. You are right.
28. They are wrong.
29. You are right.
30. They are wrong.
31. You are right.
32. They are wrong.
33. You are right.
34. They are wrong.
35. You are right.
36. They are wrong.
37. You are right.
38. They are wrong.
39. You are *so* right.
40. They are *so* wrong.

Exercises

1. If anyone talks to you, tell them they're wrong.
2. Make a list of people who think they're better than you. Call them up and tell them they're idiots.
3. Make a list of laws like theft, murder, and driving without a licence. Cross them out. They no longer exist.
4. Constantly remind yourself of your perfection. Tell yourself, "I contain all the worth in the world, therefore all others are worthless! I am all there is! I am the only company worthy of myself! I am so wonderful that there is no wonderfulness left for anyone else!"

STEP SEVEN — DENY, DENY, DENY!

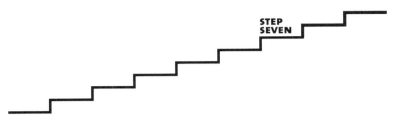

You can't handle the truth!

Congratulations! You have reached the final step of the *Seven Steps to Bliss!* program. You may feel that one more step is stupid and unnecessary. Good for you! You're starting to change. But hold on — there's just one more step for you to *Get Stupid!* And it's the most important step of all — *Deny, Deny, Deny!*

Sometimes the evidence against you is so overwhelming that it seems you must admit you are wrong — but you can't be wrong, because you are perfect and *Believe in Yourself!* How can this be resolved? Denial. Denial is the ability to make reality fit your truth. Since you are never wrong, if it seems that you're wrong, that's wrong, and that wrong must be made right by showing you were right, not wrong, because the wrong was wrong all along.

Once you have mastered denial, all things become perfect. Are you fat and out of shape? Not if you *Deny, Deny, Deny!* You're fitter than an Olympic athlete! Do you smell bad and have poor personal hygiene? No! You smell like roses. Are you a slow, stupid loser who's abandoned his children, cheated on his wife, and never done a damn thing your entire life? No, you are the king of the world!

But you can *Deny, Deny, Deny!* so much more! Are you afraid of death? Well, don't be — you will never die! You smoke? So what? Drink as much as you want, get into fights, drive drunk. You're immortal. Nothing can hurt you. Everyone else, of course, will die. So if they piss you off, who cares? Soon they'll be dead while you have eternity to smoke unfiltered cigarettes, drink absinthe, and ride motorcycles backwards.

Still need help? How about an example? Let's say you bet on a football game and your team loses. Do you pay the money? No, that is an admission that you were wrong. And you are never wrong! Therefore your team did not lose — your team won! And whoever you bet with owes *you* money. How do you defend this position? *Deny, Deny, Deny!*

Insist that your team did not lose. Oh, sure they'll bring out "evidence." Deny it all! "Those newspapers are forgeries! The people who say your team won are the same idiots who think Elvis is dead! Those highlights were filmed in the same studio where they faked the lunar landing!" If they continue to insist you lost, then sic the dogs on them; they're obviously part of the conspiracy. The world is better off without them.

Here's another example. Say you've butchered the family next door because they just wouldn't leave you alone. They kept knocking on your door to invite you over, and said "Hi" whenever you happened to venture outside. So you've chopped them up and put them in the cellar. Then, one day, the police knock on your door and ask you if you did it. "No, of course not," you say. Then they come back with a warrant and find the bodies — you're in trouble, right? Wrong. Just *Deny, Deny, Deny!* "I've never seen these people before in my life," you say when they show you pictures of your neighbours. "The bodies must have been here when I moved in," you explain as they pull the mouldy bags out of your cellar. "Don't you know that you are all merely pawns of the therapists!" you scream to the crowded courtroom as they sentence you.

See how easy it is? Now let's *Deny, Deny, Deny!* your past. Someone who used to sit behind you in math class comes to watch your trial and asks, "Hey, weren't you that loser in high school?" "No," you scream at the infidel, "I never even went to high school! I was tutored by elves. Don't you recognize the King of Glastenshite when you see him? School? Bah! I was suckled by fluffy, lactating angels and spent my childhood riding purple unicorns!" Oh, he may laugh at you, but be strong, the burdens of a king are many.

The more you *Deny, Deny, Deny!* the more you expose the great conspiracy. Everyday occurrences you once took for granted are revealed as the evil they really are. The price of gas didn't increase because of "market forces" — no, it increased because *they* want to stop you! Your pizza isn't late because of traffic — no, *they* are trying to starve you to death. Why did your dog pee on your floor? Because Oprah commanded it to! She made him eat your underwear too! Beware! Beware! They are everywhere! They control everything but you! Every single person is part of their wicked web of lies! Trust no one! Talk to no one! They are all out to get you! Every single one of them! Even the babies! Remember all I have told you and forget everything else! Even forget some of what I have told you!

You're almost done. Just finish the assignments below and then take the IQ Test again. If you pass, you're ready for Part Two, *Simplifying the*

World! If you fail, start over, and get it right this time! Good luck. I know you can *Get Stupid!*

Remember!
1. It is not enough to deceive others. You must also deceive yourself.
2. The only way someone can beat you is by cheating.
3. You are not crazy, and if someone says you are, scream in their face, "You're the one who's crazy! You're the one who speaks through my fillings! And guess what, buddy? They never landed on the moon!"
4. There is a conspiracy to get you.

5. Only you know the truth.
6. The world is a better place with you as its lord and emperor.

Exercises
1. Mount a slow campaign of terror against the house next door but never admit to it. Start by booby-trapping their porch, or have their pet "disappear." Work your way up until you're caught dumping gasoline on the veranda. Deny everything.
2. Hurt yourself badly but deny you are hurt. Do not go to the hospital or ask for help. If you die from your wounds, ignore it and carry on as usual.
3. Rip your phone out of the wall because people are hearing you through it. Smash up all your mirrors so they can't watch you anymore. Scream at the top of your lungs, "You'll never get me or my empty brain!" You may think you are alone, but they will hear you!
4. Protect your money. Empty your bank account and put all the money in an envelope. Address the envelope to: T.O. Strong, Box 48, Grim Canyon, Nevada. Bank accounts allow all your transactions to be monitored by the great conspiracy. I will hold your money for you and keep it safe. I will give it back to you when you need it. I promise.

Simplifying the World!

ALL THINGS ARE SIMPLE TO A SIMPLE MIND

Congratulations! You are now completely stupid. Can you feel the bliss? Good!

Before you climbed *The Seven Steps to Bliss!* your life was confusing and complicated, full of highs and lows, thoughts and doubts. Now it is as calm as a puddle of stagnant water. But beware, the winds of thought wish to ripple your puddle. How do you avoid these bad breezes? By cutting off the source, that's how! Burn your books! Smash up your computer! Throw your radio in the water during your next bath! You will never again be controlled by those who would make you think! But what about those rare moments of unavoidable interaction with the world? What do you do then? How do you deal with a planet you are completely ignorant of? By turning to this section, *Simplifying the World!*, that's how!

Have you heard of the Tree of Knowledge? This is a tree that the conspiracy grows to enslave you. But they haven't grown just one little tree. No, they have created an entire Forest of Falsity to confuse you. A forest that you were lured into from the moment you were born. A forest you were lost in until I found you. And to save you from ever being lost again, I have journeyed deep into this Forest of Falsity and hacked away all the lies and deceptions. Now all that is left is the Stump of Truth. It is this stump I will show you in *Simplifying the World!* A stump that will allow you to remain completely ignorant and still solve any problem.

I know reading is hard for you, so take your time, or skip this section entirely if you want, but in times of trouble I think you'll find it comforting. I have also included an inspirational saying on every page — signposts on the road of ignorance to guide you towards bliss.

Good luck, and enjoy your simple world!

Education

IT'S NEVER TOO LATE TO STOP LEARNING

Once upon a time, your mind was blissfully free. Then you went to the multi-layered system of catastrophic indoctrination known as school, which destroyed your bliss and made you think. I will now describe the various stages of the terrible system that hurt you so.

There is no inner beauty — only a collection of tissues and organs.

THE EDUCATION SYSTEM

Pre-school
When your parents became bored with you, you were sent to pre-school, where you were encouraged to share, feel, and nap. Of these three, only napping is worthwhile. Sharing and feeling, as you now know, were taught to enslave you.

Elementary School
At this level you learned the three R's of reading, riting, and rithmetic (spelling would come later). You were still told to share and feel, but napping was cruelly deleted from the curriculum. By this time the foundation for the eradication of your bliss was firmly laid.

High School
Once puberty hit, you were sent off to an adolescent concentration camp called high school to prepare you for the "real world." Here you joined a "clique" — a small group whose members show their individuality by being exactly the same as each other. This made you think you were cool and rebellious, but was actually subtle conformity training to prepare you for healing circles and group therapy.

All things are impossible when you want them to be.

Higher Education
It's possible you didn't make it this far, which is great. I was not so lucky. No, I attended college. I was only there for half an hour, but still it scarred me for life. You see, I was enrolled in something called the "liberal arts." People who study "liberal arts" get what little bliss they have left replaced with things like *German Romantic Poetry and Its Influence on the Works of the Marx Brothers*. Then they graduate and

spend the rest of their lives "finding themselves." Well, I've got news for you, bucko, you are where you are. Take your finger and put it up your nose. There you are. Right there. Nowhere else. You're not hiding on some hilltop in Tibet, you're not hanging up in the Louvre, and you're certainly not in some smelly youth hostel in Amsterdam. If only you'd spent your time trying to *Get Stupid!* you'd be happily eating cheesies in your underwear right now.

Freedom comes when you give up trying.

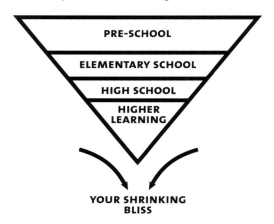

THE REMNANTS OF EDUCATION

True healing has more to do with drinking than anything else.

Although my *Seven Steps to Bliss!* have erased most of education's terrible effects on you, some traces may linger. Every now and then, just when you're feeling most blissful, a thought will pop into your head, like "Cheaters never win" or "Learning is its own reward." These are ghosts from your school years that I shall dispel forever.

"Cheaters never win"

This is a lie. *Cheaters always win!* Just look around you! Microsoft! The Kennedy family! The British monarchy! All groups who gained power and wealth through bullying and stealing. Hard work is useless! Cheating is the only way! Sure, you could spend your life working on a great invention, or you could just steal the invention from the person who invented it. Which seems easier to you? Easiest of all, of course, is to do absolutely nothing.

"Learning is its own reward"

This is like saying, "Punching yourself in the face is its own reward."

Hurting your head is hurting your head. Also, if something is its "own reward," it's probably worthless. Similar sayings, like "Being nice is its own reward" and "Square-dancing is its own reward," prove this point. The only reward you need is a big pile of ignorance!

Those who plant seeds of love reap only tears and betrayal.

TEACHERS

The educational system would never work without the loathsome cogs known as teachers. Who are these pathetic tools? They are those who have failed at everything and have settled for some twisted sense of power over the lives of little children. Nothing is more bliss-free than a teacher, as even the briefest conversation with one will prove. They are the distributors of misery, infecting generation after generation of innocent youth. And most miserable of all, of course, was Mr. Morgan....

"And just what feeling is it you're trying to convey, T.O.?" he'd say, holding up my charcoal drawing for all the class to mock.

"My hatred for you! You loathsome toad!" I'd reply.

Then I'd be sent to the office for telling the truth! Well, Mr. Morgan, what do you think of me now, huh? I didn't need to pass your stupid class. You stupid man! You stupid, stupid man! I blame you and you alone... and everyone else too! One day I'll shove those charcoal sticks up where the sun don't shine and put pastels in your nostrils! One day...

Family

IT'S ALL RELATIVES

Families are like umbilical cords — just because you're born with one, doesn't mean you should keep it. Families consist of many different types of people all bent on making your life a living hell. Here are the members:

A friend in need should be avoided at all costs.

Parents

It is your parents who first robbed you of the blissful ignorance you were born with. Who pretended to encourage you, but actually sabotaged your life so you'd end up worse than them. Who had those dinner parties where everyone put their keys in a jar while you were locked in the basement. Who abandoned you when you most needed them. Who divorced when you were a kid and forced you to call the new guy Mommy was hanging out with "Daddy"... until you pushed him down the stairs....

Do unto others whatever the hell you want.

It is best to ignore your parents. Recognize their existence only when you need money.

One day, your parents will become weak and demented. When this happens, ship them off to an old-age home. I know, it's easier to throw them out with the trash, but the conspiracy denies you this basic right. Instead, find the cheapest home you can — making sure it is inconvenient to get to — and don't visit until the last of them is about to kick the can. Then come in saying you are seeking "closure." You want to make sure they don't cut you out of the will.

Children

Children are grubby little snot-faced money-sucking monsters whose only purpose in life is to drive you mad. A child starts out as an amorphous squealing lump called a "baby." Oh sure, people will tell you that it's cute, but it *has* to be cute. If it weren't cute, it'd be killed — all it does is drool, poo, scream, and vomit.

Relief from stress comes from the elimination of concern.

But it only gets worse as it grows. Now it grabs things with its pudgy little fingers and throws them about. Then it starts talking. "No, no, no, no," it says, over and over and over again. Then you get a bright idea. Why don't you get rid of it? Well, you can't. You'd be thrown in jail! This is a good time to leave the other parent all alone with the burden. Believe me, it works.

When the creature turns thirteen, it becomes a teenager. It wears stupid clothes, mopes around, eats your food, and gives you attitude. Now you'd *really* like to kill it. But it's too late to do so safely — it's almost as big as you and downright crazy.

Finally, the teenager becomes an adult and you kick it out. You sit in your chair and think about how pleasant your life will be from now on. But it is only a dream. Your spawn continues to haunt you: asking for money, wanting you to co-sign a loan, demanding to know why you won't return its phone calls. Then it does the worst thing of all.

It goes to a therapist and blames all its problems on you. You were too distant. Oh sure, you said things like, "I had a good life until you came along." But you were just being honest. You *did* have a good life until it came along. It got in the way with its selfish needs… and you wanted a girl anyway. Now the evil therapists have it as yet another tool to use against you.

Then, one day, when you're old and grey, it ships you off to an old-age home somewhere. You never see it again until it comes seeking "closure" as you're gasping for air on a hospital bed.

The quality of my life is improved by stealing things from others.

Spouses

Marriage leaves you poor and miserable. I know, you're supposed to spend your entire life in bliss after you find "the right person." But guess what? The "right person" is *you!* Anyone else is a crowd. Oh, I'm sure you've had visions of a white picket fence, a beautiful spouse, and cute, adorable children. The truth is you will be tired and poor, your spouse will get uglier every day, and the children will drive you mad. Marriage is only good for marriage counsellors, and "counsellor" is just another word for therapist, and we all know what therapists are, don't we? Blood-sucking, mind-controlling, evil scum!

Concentrate on… umm, ah… Why am I in the kitchen?

DON'T GET MARRIED! And if you do, leave! Don't bother with a divorce; it just leaves a paper trail that makes it easy to find you. Marriage is just another scam to make you buy self-help books and cry. Don't even have relationships. Just have one-night stands, and then only when you're both too drunk to remember each other's names.

Relatives

Most people hate their relatives. Why should you have to spend time with people just because they're related to you? You're even expected to see them on your holidays! Instead of spending Christmas and Easter by yourself, thinking of how to get revenge on all those who have wronged you, you have to hang out with these assorted losers, eating turkey, looking for eggs and saying, "My, what a lovely sweater." But it's a crappy sweater, and the turkey is dry, and everyone is talking on and on and on and on as only relatives can about how smart their kids are, or if they don't have kids then dogs, and if not dogs then gold-fish. And then you scream, "You can't possibly be related to me!" And punt the turkey at Aunt Mavis.…

Relatives are useful only as a reminder that you are the only person who is any good. *Deny, Deny, Deny!* their very existence.

Money

MONEY IS THE ROOT OF ALL SPENDING

Money is the sole reason you were put on this earth. You're not here to share, or to give, or to learn, or to "do God's work." No, you're here to make and spend cash!

This contradicts all the negative things you've been told, like "The best things in life are free" and "Money can't buy you love." Let's examine these statements more closely.

"The best things in life are free"

Yeah, like poverty. See how jolly poor people are? They can't buy food, but they can still do fun things like breathe and poo. I'll let you in on a little secret — rich people are happier than poor people. You know why? Because they're rich! They can buy jet planes and powerboats and, most importantly, poor people!

"Money can't buy you love"

No, it can do better. Money can get you someone who is dependent on you and therefore more obedient than someone hanging around for "love." People don't often think about what love can get, what love can buy. A quick look at the following chart and you'll see that love is highly overrated:

Love vs. Money Chart

	LOVE	MONEY
Car	No	Yes
WWE Action Figure	No	Yes
Explosives	No	Yes
Sex	Maybe	Yes
Emotional Turmoil	Yes	No

Money wins, hands down! Love is useless while cash can get you breast implants, tartan pants, and a glowing licence-plate holder! Love sucks. Only money makes money. You do the math.

But how do you get money? Lottery tickets are a good way. Theft is another option. Try this out: get a job at a charity — like "The Semi-Starving Children of Morondavia" or "Nuns with Gout" — get people to trust you, and rise to a position where you can write the cheques. Then buy a one-way ticket to Panama and spend the rest of your life drunk and sweaty.

Others are meaningless.

If theft is too much effort, don't worry. There is an easier, legal way to live the high life: debt. Get as many credit cards as you can, take out lots of cash advances, and hide money under your mattress. Buy everything on lay-away plans. Get a house, a car, go on vacation. When you fall behind on your payments, get more credit cards and use them to pay off the others. After about three or four years, they'll stop giving you credit and ask for their stuff back. What happens when you can't pay them? Nothing! They just take what they can and leave you with anything they don't want. And you've still got all that money that was under your mattress (although you might not have the mattress). You've acted in a truly ignorant fashion and been blissfully rewarded. What can be better than that?

So what are you waiting for — go out there and steal some money! Or don't. If you're really ignorant, you'll be just as happy living in a park eating squirrels.

Health

If you want to be happy, take the red pills.

JUST DON'T DO IT!

A total lack of health is called death. Most people don't want to be dead, and a huge industry has sprung up to take advantage of this. Remember, you don't need help because nothing is wrong with you! Still, in times of weakness, you might consider "taking care of yourself." Don't do this! Here is the truth about health:

Natural Medicine
Natural therapies are based on the premise that "natural" medicine is better than "unnatural" medicine because nature is so gosh-darned nice. Well, it isn't. Nature is a dirty, grimy, grubby place. Pandas pee

in nature. Frogs fart in nature. Koalas pick their ears in nature. Monkeys scratch their crotches. Turtles lay their slimy eggs. And whales copulate. Nature is, in a word, gross.

Nature is also dangerous. Just think of some of the things that are natural. Arsenic is natural! Festering sores are natural! Falling off a cliff is natural! Broccoli is natural! Pretty scary, huh?

Tunnel vision is the only vision.

Drugs

Drugs can solve any problem. If you feel down, take an upper; if you feel up, take a downer. If you feel left, take a righter. Unlike "natural" medicines, drugs work. Want proof? Just look at Elvis. Oh, I know people say it "destroyed" him, but just remember this: ELVIS IS THE MOST SUCCESSFUL SINGER EVER! And he was on more pills than the East German woman's shot-put team. If drugs are bad, then musicians who aren't on drugs should be better than those who are. Obviously that is not the case. Have you ever heard a Christian rock band? They suck! They say they're high on God; well, God's just a stepstool compared to the rocket a bunch of good pills will give you.

Nutrition

The conspiracy even gets people to buy books to tell them how to eat! Do animals need these books? Does a pig look up the nutritional content of slop before he dives into the trough? No! No! No! But if they could teach pigs to read, you bet your booties they'd sell them books. Here's the truth. Eat whatever you want. And please, don't worry about getting fat — being fat is good. Sure, it makes you funny-looking, but fat is your insurance plan. If skinny people run out of food, they die. But fatties can live on for months! They'll make fun of you now, but just wait until your plane crashes in the Andes. We'll see who's around to eat the leftovers.

The more you give, the less you have.

"But shouldn't I at least eat natural foods?" you ask. Nope. Why would you eat something that developed haphazardly when you could eat something that has been created specifically to be eaten? Genetically altered foods get better every day! Soon you'll be able to buy bite-sized cows, potatoes that grow pre-fried, and brightly coloured cubes and triangles like they have on *Star Trek*. We already have Pop-Tarts — now that's good eating.

So avoid anything natural, eat lots of Pop-Tarts, and don't trust skinny people.

Smoking

Smokers are the lepers of the modern age. They have been driven out of doors like disobedient dogs that have pooed on their master's bed. But smokers haven't pooed anywhere. They are merely unfortunate victims of the conspiracy. Even the good names of tobacco multinationals have been tarnished. It aches my heart to see those poor executives — some of the last ignorant people left — defend themselves in inquiry after inquiry, desperately trying to get the truth heard. But nobody listens.

The truth is, smoking is good for you! It relieves stress and makes you look cool. And, as we all know, stress and not looking cool are the top two killers in the world today. Not only that, but smoking is very, very tasty.

Ignore the toughest problems first.

Did you know that children are banned from buying cigarettes? Banned! How are those kids going to relieve stress? How are they going to look cool?

Don't let the conspiracy win! Smoke! In restaurants, in airplanes, in emergency wards at hospitals! And if they try to make you stop, if they try to deny you your right to look cool and relaxed, tell them that an unjust law is no law at all and punch them in the face!

Alcohol

Alcohol is good. It makes other people briefly interesting and gives you insight into all the problems of the world. It also helps make your liver big and strong by giving it a vigorous workout. Remember, reality is an illusion caused by lack of booze.

There's no need to argue when you're packing heat.

Exercise

Exercise kills. Joggers drop dead, cyclists get hit by cars, and swimmers drown. This fact alone should discourage you from ever doing it. After all, your body has only so much energy, and if you use it up now, you'll have nothing left in five years. Besides, exercise wastes time. Why would you jog when you could be home drinking, smoking, popping pills, and watching TV?

Exercise also makes you look silly — running around like some animal! We are on top of the food chain! We don't need to run or jump or swim. We just need to pick up the phone and call the pizza guy. In the future we will lose all our bones and muscles except for the one finger to press the button for auto-dial.

Politics

A POLITICAL PARTY ISN'T MUCH FUN

Annoying people end up in power because no one else can be bothered.

These irritating people are arranged differently, depending on what political system you live under. Here they are:

Democracy

You are not part of the circle of life. You are a straight line going on forever.

Most modern countries are democracies. A democracy is run by the people for the people. Sounds good, doesn't it? Now, take a look around you. What do you see? Losers! Other people are losers! They don't understand you! All they want to do is take away your fun! Would you let the guy who works in the coffee shop — who fills your cup to the rim so you have to sip some coffee off to make room for the milk and then burn your tongue because it's too hot, making you wince in pain and drop your coffee on your crotch so everyone thinks you've peed your pants — running your life? Do you want all those old farts — who want you to pay more taxes so they can have nice new medical equipment that lets them die more slowly — running your life? Do you want that big-haired, slack-jawed woman with twenty-nine kids — who wants you to pay more taxes so she can stay home and feed her pack of vermin — running your life?

Be more like a child: greedy, self-centred, and immune from prosecution.

In a democracy they do. The fix is in! All those unhappy, unblissful, mind-controlled idiots vote for the conspiracy's candidate. Which isn't surprising, because they're all the conspiracy's candidate! If you're living in a democracy, good luck. Ignore the rules as best you can: don't vote, don't pay taxes, and don't obey any laws. You're not a loser — *they* are!

Communism

Communism is pretty passé, but there are still a couple of unfashionable countries that use it. The point of communism is to make people equal by taking away everything. Where does the stuff go? To the politicians, of course. Once this is accomplished, they set up a system where nothing is ever produced, ensuring miserable equality forever.

Dictatorship

In a dictatorship, one person has absolute power and everyone else just tries to avoid execution. Dictatorship is a whimsical form of government based on one person's vision. If the dictator doesn't like moustaches, then everyone with moustaches is beheaded and shaved. If the dictator likes *Three's Company*, he devotes the entire nation's resources to bringing back the original cast for a reunion show, which is quite expensive considering that John Ritter must be revived from the dead. Children starve, hospitals close, while the dictator delights in a whole new series of hilarious misunderstandings.

Never drown unwanted kittens. It's easier to bake them.

Mousetocracy

These countries are ruled by a giant mouse with a squeaky, effeminate voice. For a long time there were just two of these nations (both in North America), but they have since spread to Europe and Asia. Mousetocracies have hefty border charges and their economies are based on selling T-shirts and dolls. Unlike most nations, you can actually meet the ruler when you visit. He will not talk to you, but he will wave and give half-hearted hugs, although there are rumours he uses body doubles. People who spread these rumours are often found dead later, their bloated bodies washed up on shore with *Treasure Planet* merchandise shoved down their throats.

The power you need exists in the outlets on your walls.

Fashion

NO SHOES, NO SHIRT, JUST UNDERWEAR

Underwear is good enough.

The fashion fascists want to keep this fact from you. Why? Because they want to sell you cummerbunds and skirts and blouses and gloves and shoes and pants — all absolutely useless! If you have two pairs of underwear, you're set. One pair is enough, but it makes laundry awkward, especially if you have to go to a laundromat.

Dare to do nothing!

There are many good reasons to wear only underwear. First off, it decreases the chance of getting stains on your clothes. You usually spill coffee down your shirt, don't you? Well, if you're not wearing a shirt, it's not going to stain, is it? Then you don't have to wash it. And if you don't have to wash it, then you don't have to pay for washing it. And that means you have more money for beer and guns — two items that accessorize underwear surprisingly well. And underwear *is* fashionable. Many people who have managed to *Get Stupid!* have appeared on television shows such as *Cops* wearing only their underwear. If it's good enough for national television, then it must be good enough for you.

Now, I'm not saying you should ignore fashion altogether. You should still watch fashion TV shows — they often have hot-looking naked people on — but turn off the sound. The reporters are very annoying and do not shut up. They'll describe the colour red a thousand different ways without ever using the word "red." Then they'll talk about some colour being the new black, or the new white, or that tartan is actually the new orange, and that short is the new tall, but only in Milan. It's very confusing and will hurt your head.

Another fashion excess is shoes. You may remember back when you actually went outside that every other store in the world sells shoes. Why is this? How many feet do you have? Two. So how many shoes do you need? NONE! You don't need any! Believe it or not, feet are meant to be walked on! Try it sometime. Walk around without shoes.

Feet work fine! Who thought squeezing your toes into a triangle and then putting your heel ten inches off the ground, balanced on a spike, was a good idea anyway? I still have bunions from wearing them. How many animals wear shoes? NONE! (Oh, yeah, I know some horses wear shoes, but that's because evil, greedy blacksmiths make them.) So why do we wear them? Because the conspiracy makes us, so they can track us with the transmitters embedded in them. They know where you are and what you're doing!

So throw out your clothes, burn your shoes, and slip into a pair of underwear.

It's all the fashion you need.

The Arts

HOBBIES FOR THE USELESS

I'm sure you've heard, "Society doesn't do enough to support the arts." Who says this? Why, artists of course: money-grubbing loafers who want you to pay them to make self-indulgent crap. Why would you support them? They never support anything *you* like. Would they buy you a bull for a bullfight? No, they'd say it was cruel. Have you ever sat through modern dance? How cruel is that?

Here's how art works. The government takes money from you and gives it to a bunch of whiny, self-centred no-talents whose only real skill is filling out grant applications, and in return you get stuff that you don't want and can't afford anyway because the government has taken all your money to fund them. And what is the purpose of art? Is it supposed to make you happy? No, it is supposed to challenge you, to make you think and feel! It is designed to destroy your bliss! To drag you from the peace of ignorance into the turmoil of discovery! To make you miserable! And you're *paying* for this!

Avoid art always, and destroy it when you can. But you are probably so ignorant now that you can't recognize what you are avoiding. To help out, I will describe the many faces of this evil to you.

Opera
Opera is the art of big fat men and big fat women singing while they die. Operas are so stupid that they can't be sung in English, and are instead sung in foreign languages like French, Italian, and Eskimo.

Classical Music
All classical music was written by composers who died hundreds of years ago from syphilis. The music is played by a bunch of people in cheap tuxedos who don't have the gumption to start up their own bands.

Ballet
Ballet is dancing at its dullest. Real dancing — such as belly dancing and lap dancing — is exciting. There's no excitement in ballet.

Painting

Painting involves taking little blobs of paint and putting them on the canvas to make a picture that still isn't as good as one you can take with a disposable camera.

Theatre

Theatre is like bad television, except you can't turn the channel. Once it starts, you're stuck. The most annoying thing about theatre is that when you talk out loud, like you do at home, people "shhhh" you. Every time you scream out, "BORING! BORING!" someone gives you the evil eye. And this is an "art form" that supposedly encourages freedom of expression. Well, if it's so goddamn free, I should be able to yell, "The actors suck!" and "It'd be better with a lesbian love scene!" Do yourself a favour. Just watch television. Or rent a video with lesbian love scenes.

I have not failed — I have succeeded without success.

Charcoal Drawings

This is a technique used by teachers to destroy students. Somehow the teacher's favourites always get an A plus, while those of us with real talent fail.

Science

BEWARE THE NERDS!

Science and Art are often considered opposites, but they are closer than most people think, for they have one thing in common — you should ignore them. Now, I don't want you to become one of those Amish weirdos with their horses, scraggly beards, and lack of television. No, I just want you to not *think* about science. Because even though science is bad, it occasionally creates useful things like firearms and processed cheese. So, by all means, use what you want, just don't think about how it works.

It is easier to adjust the scale than to lose the weight.

Science is made by scientists. Do you remember those nerdy kids you used to beat up in high school? Now they're scientists! Oh, they think they're better than you with their jobs and dental plans, but they're still the same losers they were back then. If you find a scientist, give him a wedgie, or face-flush him in a toilet, to remind him he's still a loser. If he happens to have a lunch, steal it.

Why do scientists get paid so much? Because they are vital to the conspiracy's plans, that's why. You see, scientists create theories. These theories are then given to teachers who use them to torture students and make them think. Most devious of all, these theories aren't even true! If you never understood high-school physics, it wasn't because you couldn't — no, it was because you instinctively knew how ridiculous these theories are. To prove my point I will show you the truth behind some of the theories you were taught.

Tolerance is for the weak.

The Theory of Gravity

Hundreds of years ago, this guy called Newton saw an apple fall to the ground. Then he created the theory of gravity, which is: when apples fall from trees, they fall down instead of up. This is hardly revolutionary stuff. Where else is the apple going to go? Maybe if there was a big updraft or a vacuum cleaner or something, it'd go into the sky. Or perhaps a large bird could carry it off. The reason Newton is so well respected was that he then created an "equation" that supposedly predicted which way an apple would fall off a tree. And just what is an equation? Well, it's some mumbo jumbo that scientists say to convince you that they know what they're doing. It's like a second-rate magician saying "Abracadabra!" In reality the scientists just make up whatever number comes into their heads. But of course they pretend that the equation actually works and that the reason you can't figure it out is because you're a big dummy.

Only laugh at others.

Newton made many more theories during his career — all as ridiculous as the first — but his only discovery of any real worth was the Fig Newton.

The Theory That the Earth Is Round

I'm not sure who came up with this lie but it's been around for years. If the earth were round, we'd fall off, wouldn't we? Newton's apples would fly off into space! All of Australia's funny-looking animals would drop straight off into nowhere. If it were round, then how come maps are flat? How come? Answer me *that*!

The Theory of Evolution

This theory states that animals developed from other animals as part of the "survival of the fittest." Ha! Look at the people around you. Do they look fit? How do you explain Florida? All those old fat people should have been knocked out of evolutionary contention long ago. If evolution was true, then fitter people would have come along, eaten them, stolen their golf carts, and taken over their condos and time-shares. And how do you explain the sloth? How fit is that lazy, good-for-nothing critter? No, evolution is a crock. "Well," you may ask, "then how did we get here? What is our purpose?" I'll give you some simple advice on the meaning of life — shut up and eat some cheesies!

The Theory of Relativity

This theory states that your relatives age at different rates depending on how fast they're running. Although I'll admit that some of my relatives age more quickly than others, I'm pretty sure it's not because of how fast they're going. My aunt Hilda, who's sixty but looks ninety, actually walks rather quickly, while I know this one old guy who looks twenty years younger than his age who can barely walk because of his gimpy leg. I just can't see the connection.

Einstein, the guy who came up with this theory, was so popular that when he died people took his brain out and put it in a jar. There are rumours that at this very moment his brain is co-writing songs with Elvis for a big comeback album.

The Environment

GIVE A HOOT — POLLUTE!

Before you achieved your bliss, you were made to doubt your natural desire to pollute. The hippies (pawns of the conspiracy) made you do this, because when you doubt, you think! But when you *Get Stupid!* you learn we should not be protecting the environment — no, we should be attacking it!

Recycling

Recycling is unnatural. You don't recycle hair, do you? Or nails? Or snot? No, once they're out of your body, they're gone. So why would you recycle things? We should be making *more* disposable items, not fewer. We should have disposable socks, disposable refrigerators, and disposable children! We should never have to touch the same thing twice! Garbage heaps should be viewed as the magnificent achievements they are and tower as high as the Andes! That way we could climb to the top and look out at the wonderful progress we have made.

If you don't have a job, you'll never work a day in your life.

Pollution

Animals mark their territory with scent, but we mark ours with pollution. Pollution lets animals know who's the boss. Most animals, when they discover they're on land that doesn't belong to them, feel bad and die of guilt.

Endangered Species

Just as someone is bulldozing the last piece of the useless rain forest, some hippie will yell, "What about the black-toed three-legged weed-hopper? That's their only habitat!" Well, screw them! I've been evicted lots of times, and you know what? I moved on. I found a new "habitat." Animals can do the same. And if they can't hack it, they deserve to die. Do we really want to encourage loser species? Do we want to save the pandas who are too lazy to get off their big hairy black-and-white asses? Do we need more koalas who only eat one type of plant? And who will miss the butt-ugly condors?

You are always right.

Why do people even *care* about nature? Nature doesn't give a rat's ass about us. What with all the hurricanes and volcanoes and plagues of locusts, it can be argued that "Mother Nature" has it coming. It's time for some payback. Instead of trying to stop species from falling into extinction, we should be giving them an extra push! Cut down the forests! Burn more coal! Coat the planet in DDT. That'll show those animals.

Global Warming

The conspiracy wants us to believe that the planet is getting warmer because of pollution. Lies, lies, and more lies. They just want to sell you more books and energy-efficient light bulbs. And what if it were true? Wouldn't it be a good thing? Sure all those places that are already hot would get hotter, but just crank up the air conditioning.

And think of all the cold land that would warm up. Siberia would become a tropical paradise filled with fat, tanned Russians throwing beach parties. If that doesn't sound like fun, I don't know what does.

Travel

ALL JOURNEYS START WITH A SINGLE STEP, BUT IT'S EASIER STAYING HOME

Don't go anywhere. And I don't just mean "Don't go to Spain" or "Don't visit your mom in Duluth," I mean "Don't even walk to the bathroom." Instead, buy some adult underwear, place a ten-gallon drum of jujubes beside your La-Z-Boy, and sit.

If you absolutely have to go somewhere, get it over with quickly. I know you've spent your whole life hearing that "Travel broadens the mind." But there is no reason to visit different places. You've seen rocks before, right? You've seen plants before, right? You've seen people before, right? Then why would you go halfway around the world to see stuff you've seen a million times before, slightly rearranged?

Travel is pointless. On top of that, travel is annoying. Even worse, travel makes you think. I'm sure you'll agree there's no good way to travel.

Plane

Air travel is supposed to be fast when, in fact, it is the slowest of all forms of transportation. But how can that be when planes travel at hundreds of miles an hour? Let me explain.

First you need to take a cab to the airport, which is always located in the most inaccessible part of the city. This takes an hour. Then you check in and go through security, which takes two hours. Then your flight gets delayed, and another couple hours pass. Finally, you board the plane, which proceeds down the runway. Then the plane stops. And sits. And all the time some old lady is yammering about how she's going to visit her cousin in Kelowna, and all you want to do is jam the free travel magazine down her throat, but you figure she'll probably pass away sometime in the next hour anyway. Suddenly, the pilot comes on the intercom announcing, "There's some unexpected delay, so it appears we have to go back to the gate where we will treat you rudely and give you as little information as possible." And that's what they do.

So you're back in the airport again, sitting in the bar drinking $8 bottles of Bud Lite and waiting for something to happen. Nothing does. The sun goes down. The sun rises. You are informed that your airline has gone bankrupt. You can't take a cab because you've spent all your money buying Bud Lite. You're stuck. Trapped in the airport. Forever. You become a subhuman beast, living off of half-eaten donuts and lemon rinds from abandoned gin and tonics. You scrounge around the terminal, day after day, month after month, waiting for someone to drop a boarding pass so that you can go somewhere, anywhere. But it never happens. Years go by. You die of old age and are recycled with the newspapers.

Put off everything.

Don't travel by plane.

Train

Trains are totally useless. They only travel where there are train tracks! How many places do you want to go to that are actually on train tracks? None! There are no buildings on train tracks because there are trains on train tracks.

Don't travel by train.

Boat

Cramped city-dwellers, who want to get away from it all, get on a boat with two thousand people they'd never associate with on land, and sail around in circles. While on the boat, they drink, gamble, shop, and are subjected to "entertainment" provided by cynical, bored, burnt-out losers with no taste, even less pride, and viciously persistent cocaine habits. Actually, this form of travel is pretty ignorant, especially if there's a casino on board. Just make sure you drink a lot.

Memories are like warts — they're best burned off.

Car

Cars are cool, no doubt about it. But they are not meant to be used as transportation. Cars are toys meant to race around streets, cut off other cars, and crush pedestrians. You don't travel in them. You drive them around, and then you go home.

Don't travel by car.

Sports

IT'S ALL FUN AND GAMES WHEN SOMEONE LOSES AN EYE!

Early to bed and early to rise makes a man miss late-night television.

Sports are for watching, not for doing. Just like the movies. You wouldn't watch *Star Wars* and then go out and make your own sequel, would you? So why would you watch a basketball game and then go off and play it yourself? Sports should be left to the drugged-up pros. And besides, the more time you spend playing sports, the less time you can spend watching them.

Why would I encourage you to watch sports when I've been telling you to ignore the world? Because sports are truly ignorant. They reward people with useless skills, waste huge amounts of time and money, and turn otherwise "intelligent" people into thoughtless animals. This is good! So pick a team and live through them. Make their success the only thing that matters in your life. Paint your stomach, get drunk, and yell at the TV. Can you feel the bliss?

Now, not all things called "sports" are actually sports. Some are just activities. How can you tell the difference? A sport is a pointless exercise where people get hurt, while an activity is just a pointless exercise. Remember, it's all fun and games until someone loses an eye — then it's a sport. Curling, for example, is not a sport. You never hear of "career-ending" curling injuries, do you? The worst thing curlers get is a rash from rubbing their big chubby thighs together as they sweep.

You are perfect. The flaws are elsewhere.

I know this is confusing, and I promised that you wouldn't have to think, so I have conveniently separated the "sports" from the "not sports."

NOT SPORTS

Figure Skating

Figure skating sucks. The most exciting move is a spin. A spin! Or they jump! Well, whoop-tee-dee, isn't that exciting! And they're always dressed like low-rent showgirls, wearing costumes that were bought at one of Liberace's yard sales. If they all did their routines at the same time, like some sort of battle royal on ice, then maybe I'd watch it, or if they made better use of the blades on their feet, or better yet if they did it carrying machetes! Now we're getting somewhere.

66

Darts

Darts is a wonderfully ignorant activity, but there is just not enough violence to make it a sport. It needs some aggression. I'd make the competitors *wear* the dartboards. That way you could win by scoring points, or make the other guy concede by throwing a dart in his eye! I'm surprised no one has thought of this.

To be grateful is to be wrong.

Curling

In curling the elements of a sport are in place but not used. If the brooms were employed as offensive weapons, if the rocks were thrown at opponents, and if the teams brawled, you'd have something worthwhile. But instead we get a bunch of middle-aged losers sliding slowly down the ice, thinking about the two beers they'll have after the game, and how late they paid the babysitter to stay.

SPORTS

Hockey

Hockey is the best of the team sports (except for tag-team wrestling, which it often resembles). Unlike in most sports, the rules are seldom used. According to the rules, hockey is about skating, passing, and scoring. Fortunately it is actually about tripping, spearing, and fighting. One of the wonders of hockey is the interesting ways people can get hurt. Their heads get smashed on the ice, pucks knock out teeth, and sometimes one guy will just whack the other guy on the head with a big stick! And then they fight… on ice! What could be more ignorant than a couple of guys with bulky equipment and no leverage standing on ice trying to beat each other up? And in the rare event that someone actually tries to play the games by the rules, he's roughed up and called a suck. It's a truly beautiful sport.

Never try. Never think. Never start.

Auto Racing

Many people don't consider auto racing a proper sport because it's more about the car than the person. This is crap. There is perhaps no more ignorant sport than auto racing. Here's how it works. A bunch of drivers get into really fast cars and drive around and around in circles. Everyone waits for them to crash and, when they do, everyone pretends to be horrified, but really, that's what they were hoping for the entire time. Sometimes the drivers even die! Even better, occasionally the cars go careening into the stands and kill the spectators! Now, that's a sport!

There is a great conspiracy to bring you down.

Wrestling

By wrestling, I mean professional wrestling, not that creepy, ass-grabbing, Greco-Roman stuff at the Olympics. Watching wrestling helps you maintain a high level of ignorance as long as you remember one thing: WRESTLING IS REAL! People say it's fake to appease the sissies who think it's a bad influence on their kids. This is silly; wrestling is one of the few positive influences left for our children. Where else can they learn that thinking is unimportant, that people are mere stereotypes, that women should wear very little clothing and have artificial breasts? Not in school, that's for sure. There they learn to hug — which is *not* the kind of physical contact they should be learning about. They should be learning to do flying elbows and atomic drops. If you have children, or even know children, please make them watch some wrestling. It is nothing less than your duty.

Ignorance is the only flower that blossoms on barren soil.

When you reach for the stars, you put out your back.

Sports	Not Sports
Hockey	Curling
Wrestling	Ballet
Car racing	Figure skating
Football	Billiards
Gladiatorial combat	Badminton
Boxing	Tennis
Cock fights	Scrabble (non-contact)
Competitive head-butting	Hopscotch
Scrabble (full contact)	Newspaper reading

Foreign Lands

THERE'S A WHOLE WORLD TO IGNORE!

You may be surprised that there are other countries besides the one you live in (or that you even live in a country), but do not worry, they are of absolutely no importance. You don't need to know anything about them, and you should never visit them. I will now briefly describe all the nations of the earth so that you have no reason to go to them. When you are finished reading, forget they ever existed.

France

France is full of French people, who instead of speaking English speak some foreign language, which I'm pretty sure is Polish. They are so primitive that they have not yet invented sliced bread and are forced to walk about the streets carrying gigantic bread sticks. Their capital city, Duluth, features the Eiffel Tower, which is constructed entirely out of Popsicle sticks.

All the beautiful things in the world aren't worth the snot in your nose.

England

You'd think with a name like England they'd speak English, but they don't. They all talk funny and hate each other. Food is especially terrible in England, as it was only recently discovered. If you want to simulate a trip to England, get dressed in your most uncomfortable clothes, stand in the shower, turn the water on a low cool spray, punch yourself in the face, and complain.

Africa

Africa's largest industry is the production of *National Geographic* television specials featuring fanciful animals like elephants and hippopotamuses. Do not be fooled! They are not real! They are actors in funny suits! Next time you see a *National Geographic* special, look for the zippers.

Antarctica

Antarctica is ruled by penguins.

China

There is so little room in China that people are forced to live inside of other people. Chinese families are allowed only one child. If a mother gives birth to a second, she must put it back in again. The Chinese people speak a language called "French," which even they do not understand. China's greatest building is a really big wall. Some people think it's "great," but it's really pretty mediocre.

Belittle the small.

Russia

Russia used to be called the Soviet Union but lost that name in a hand of poker. Russians excel at sports, particularly alcoholism. Russia is large and cold, like a giant walk-in freezer with nothing but frozen beets inside. Many countries have tried to invade Russia, but when they finally got there and saw the place, they grew depressed and died. Russia used to be a communist country but recently changed to democracy to become poorer.

Sweden

Soar like a bird and get hit by a plane.

Sweden is on trial at the World Court for crimes against humanity because they created ABBA. Everything in Sweden is built out of IKEA furniture and the entire country can be disassembled with an Allen key, provided you can find one that fits.

Germany

For years, the Germans tried to take over the world because they were sick and tired of living in Germany with all those Germans. Until recently, Germany was divided into East and West by the Great Wall of China, but it finally fell over due to lack of maintenance. Both East and West were disappointed to find Germans on the other side.

Australia

Australia is a large, barren country filled with incomprehensible people and stupid-looking animals. Because of a lack of precipitation, Australians live off a diet consisting solely of Vegemite and beer.

South America

If you can dream it, you can't do it.

South America is full of forgettable countries like Peru, Ecuador, and Taiwan. Some parts of South America are mountainous and others are not, but all parts are south. South America is full of ruins from cultures that existed thousands of years ago and then "mysteriously" disappeared. There is no mystery here. The cultures never existed. The ruins are made of Styrofoam.

Mexico

The greatest of all Mexicans was Speedy Gonzales, a plucky little mouse who could run very quickly. Unfortunately Speedy once called Mickey names over a bottle of tequila and disappeared.

Canada

The population of Canada is twenty-nine, yet it takes up fully two-thirds of the earth's available land. Canada has abundant natural resources and is the world's No. 1 exporter of game-show hosts.

United States of America

The United States of America is the world's largest shopping mall. Americans are staunch defenders of free speech as long as you agree with them on everything. There were plans to put up a giant dome around the U.S., but it was abandoned when they discovered it would make it impossible for them to share their pollution with the rest of the world.

Everything looks up when you're in the gutter.

Map of the World

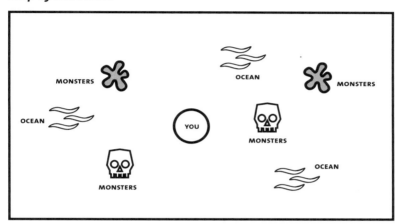

Sex

ALL THE LOVE YOU NEED IS IN THE PALM OF YOUR HAND!

Sex is the awkward exchange of bodily fluids between two (or more) creatures. It is a primitive instinct (like sandwich-making) and is perfectly harmless in its basic form.

When your heart is your guide, misery is your destination.

Unfortunately, it has been corrupted. The forces of evil don't even want you to call it sex — no, they want you to call it "making love." Because once you think sex and love are related, you will never be free. You'll buy cards, and flowers, and, worst of all, self-help books on relationships! The next thing you know you're in couples' therapy and — boom! — your life is over. And all you wanted was a quick romp.

Keep sex primitive. Do what the animals do (although I don't mean this literally). A cat raising her behind, wailing loudly, then getting tackled by a team of horny toms, is not "making love." They don't go out for coffee to find common interests. The boy cats don't bring the girl cats $30 bottles of wine and chocolates in pink packaging. They don't eat at some restaurant with bad lighting and free breadsticks. No, it's just in and out and done!

Insects are even better role models. Look at the praying mantis. The male doesn't even stick around for a nap. You know why? Because the female will eat his head! Just like human females! They want your brain! Well, you can't have it! It's mine! Run while you can! Run from the cranium-sucking monsters!

You cannot plough with a tuba.

Who to Have Sex With

Yourself. You know where you've been, you can't get yourself pregnant, and you're unlikely to eat your own head (it's physically challenging). But what if you *need* to have sex with someone else? *Deny, Deny, Deny!* When the urge comes, repress it. If it becomes unbearable, ease the pressure by lashing out at others. If this fails, and you absolutely must have sex with someone, just remember: never have sex with someone you are in a relationship with! Why? Because the only reason they're in the relationship is to destroy you. It will start with some noncommittal sex and you'll think, "Why don't we do that again?" So you do. Then again and again and again. Then, one night, your sex partner rolls over and says, "What are you thinking?" You say, "Nothing!" And then your partner says, "Don't you love me?" And you say, "Of course not." Then the crying starts. And all those feelings you got rid of sneak right back in!

Start nowhere. Go nowhere.

So get yourself a doll. Give it a sexy name like Plasticia, Goddess of My Loins, and go to town. You won't need cards or feelings. Just a good set of lungs or a bicycle pump.

Birth Control

When you have sex by yourself, birth control is unnecessary and annoying. When you have sex with another person, however, it is unnecessary and annoying. What could possibly happen? So you get a kid — who cares? Children are truly evil, but if you get rid of it quickly enough you can emerge relatively unscathed. Just run as fast as your feet can carry you. And if you're the mother, just sell it on eBay. There are people who will pay for babies. Good money too! It could be just what you need every nine months or so, especially if all your credit cards have been cancelled.

Cooking

IF THE FOOD FITS, EAT IT!

Because of your hard-earned ignorance, you'd expect that cooking would be a chore and your culinary choices would be limited. But *Get Stupid!* actually increases your food options. You can now eat with a total disregard for your health. Expiry dates are meaningless! You can drink two-month-old milk directly from the container! Or the cow! Likewise, refrigeration and heating are now unnecessary. Food is best at the temperature you find it. Besides, your electricity was probably cancelled long ago. If you have a fridge, it is still useful, though. Throw whatever food you buy (or steal) inside and forget it until you're hungry. Then, every time you eat becomes an adventure. Who knows what you'll find! Green turkey, furry mayonnaise, your dead dog... A whole world of excitement awaits you!

What to eat?
It's best to eat processed foods: Spam, Cheez Whiz, extremely white bread, and Pizza Pops are all solid choices. Eating processed food eliminates the need for your body to process the stuff itself, saving you time and energy. Whole-grain foods should be especially avoided. Not only are they completely indigestible, but fibre clogs up your system, making it hard to ram more food down your throat.

Another tip: don't eat vegetables. They're bad for you. Just look at vegetarians. They never look healthy. And they're whiny too. Always complaining about "the man" and how it's mean to eat animals. Well, if we didn't eat them, do you know who would? Animals! Animals eat other animals all the time! They're cannibals! What do you think about that, hippie? And besides, we invented most of the animals we eat. We gave them life. Cows wouldn't survive ten minutes in the wild. A large raccoon could kill one. It's a perfectly fair trade. We grant pigs and cows life and, in return, we take it away later. But the vegetarians would rather pigs and cows never existed. You tell me who the real animal lover is! Besides, meat is tasty. Even vegetarian animals taste good.

How to eat it?
Table manners are a lie. Every cent spent on forks, knives, spoons, and napkin rings goes directly to the conspiracy. But it's not just your money they're after. They want you to think. That's why place settings at fancy restaurants consist of three forks, eight spoons, and various unidentifiable utensils. They're forcing you to figure out which one goes with which food. Then, when you use the wrong fork, people laugh at you, and you feel bad. Now they've got you to feel too!

What to do? Use your hands. Even with the soup! It makes everything easy; you don't need to set the table, you don't need to clean the table, you don't even need a table! Eat over the sink. Or eat right in the fridge. Just grab it and swallow… don't even chew! It just wastes time. Besides, you shouldn't even have teeth… they're a creation of the conspiracy! We're not born with them. So where do they come from? Dentists! That sound you heard under your bed as a kid wasn't a monster; it was a dentist, waiting for you to go to sleep so he could slip teeth into your mouth! Because once you have teeth they own you! They train you to brush and floss, and to see them four times a year so they can rob you blind and put that goo in your mouth and tell you to bite down hard. That goo is mind-control goo! Free your mind, get rid of your teeth! Pull them out or bash them on a rock!

Recipes
You may have no mind, no heart, and no teeth, but it's still fun to eat. Here are some of my favourite recipes, to help you out.

LUNCHEON MEAT SURPRISE

A delightful meal any time of day

Prep time   8 seconds

Ingredients Two pieces of bread

Meat (any kind)

Directions

Go to fridge. Search until you find something that might be meat.
Put it between the pieces of bread. Put in your mouth. Swallow.

Chef's Secret!

A delightful variation is the open-face luncheon-meat surprise. This
requires only one piece of bread and works best when the meat is
placed on top.

CHEEZ WHIZ ON SAUSAGE

A classic

Prep time   4 seconds

Ingredients Cheez Whiz

Sausage

Directions

Get a sausage. I don't care how. Grab an open bottle of Cheez
Whiz (it is always best to open things as soon as you buy them to
save time later). Dip sausage in Cheez Whiz. Put in mouth.
Swallow.

Chef's Secret!

Everything tastes good dipped in Cheez Whiz!

BATTERED VERMIN

Food on the run

Prep time Depends on vermin

Ingredients Vermin

Shotgun pellets

Directions

Grab your gun. Wait quietly in kitchen for the vermin that live in your hovel to come out. Shoot until dead. Kick. Repeat. Put in mouth. Swallow.

Chef's Secret!

For variety, kill vermin in different ways. Some ideas: crush underfoot; strangle with piano wire; poison.

PEANUT BUTTER FINGERS

A wonderful sticky treat

Prep time 3 seconds

Ingredients Peanut Butter

Whatever's on your fingers

Directions

Grab tub of peanut butter (which, as stated above, should already be open). Put fingers in peanut butter and scoop out. Put in mouth. Swallow. Repeat until satisfied.

Chef's Secret!

If you have a really big tub of peanut butter, you can put your whole head in and eat directly with your mouth, saving valuable seconds.

PIZZA

Always a favourite

Prep time   30 minutes or it's free

Ingredients Pizza

Directions

Pick up phone. Call pizza place. Tell them to send you a pizza.
When door rings, answer wearing your underwear, with your dog by
your side and a gun in your hand. Tell them, "I think you're late."
They won't argue with you. Place pizza in mouth. Swallow.

Chef's Secret!

You can order more than one pizza. With one call, you can get
enough food for a month!

Gardening and Lawn Care

PRUNE YOUR GREEN THUMB

At first glance, gardening seems delightfully stupid. It is an utterly
futile activity that wastes time and numbs the mind. But beware!
Beneath its apparently benign surface lies a whole universe of thinking. Gardening, you see, involves a great deal of knowledge. Different
plants must be placed in different places at different times according
to different situations. Just learning all their names takes thought.
And then, once you've learned them, you have to learn them all over
again in Latin. There you were, blissfully playing in the mud, and now
they've got you learning Latin! The solution, of course, is to pave over
your garden. But, if you absolutely feel the need to garden, limit yourself to the following plants:

1. Weeds — Weeds are great because you don't have to do anything — just sit back and watch them grow. Let them get as high as possible, then light them on fire.

2. Man-eating plants — These are a great source of death and amusement. Unfortunately, no matter how hard I've looked, I've been unable to find any. How can you call yourself a "garden centre" if you're lacking the only plant worth buying? Move out the pansies and bring me my man-eating plants!

Gardeners

Even worse than gardening are gardeners. Gardeners lurk in the yard, waiting for you to come out so they can talk to you about annuals and loam and the latest advances in mulch. Then they give you zucchini. Somehow they grow tons of it in a tiny backyard patch. What do they use it for? To control your mind, that's what. They say, "Hey, want some zucchini? You could put it in a sauce or maybe make bread." It's a trap! Once you take the zucchini they have an excuse to talk to you. "Hey, did you make any sauce yet?" they'll say. And the next thing you know you're over at their place swapping recipes, having tea and zucchini bread. Soon you find yourself growing zucchini as well, your blissful life a thing of the past! Don't let this happen to you! Torch your neighbour's garden or feed him to your man-eating plant.

Lawn Care

Now that we've handled the garden, let's move on to your lawn. Why do you have one? What does it do for you? After all, it's a lot of work — you have to weed it, and fertilize it, and cut it... or do you? What if you just let it grow? What would happen then? Wonderful things, that's what. When you let your lawn grow, it provides cover from the prying eyes of the world. Your pit bull can hide in it and attack trespassers, you can hide in it with your gun, and no one will ever see your man-eating plant before it's at least grabbed an arm. So let it grow! If you want to help it out, you can always add old cars, garbage, and threatening signs. A lawn says a lot about the person living there and you want yours to scream, "What the hell are you looking at!"

Farewell for Now

IT'S BEEN GOOD NOT GETTING TO KNOW YOU!

We've had a wonderful time, but now that the bliss has been restored to your delicate head, it's time for me to go. But remember, I still need your help to fight the forces of evil. How can you help? By doing nothing. Don't think, don't feel, don't wash. Simply be stupid in the most ignorant way possible.

If you are still having doubts, if you are still thinking and feeling even after reading this book, then screw you! I did what I could. I gave you a way out, but no! You'd rather support *them* in their attempt to destroy me! I hope you spontaneously die this very moment, or at a moment not too far away.

To finish this book, I'm adding some letters I've received from people like you who have used my program to become more blissful. These are — Did you hear that? These are letters that they — There it is again! It's them, isn't it? Why didn't you tell me? You're one of them, aren't you? Mr. Morgan put you up to this, didn't he? I should have known. You'll never get me! Never! My stupidity is my own! You will not put things in my precious mind! Mommy? Mommy? Where are you, Mommy?

T.O. Strong

P.S. — If you have not sent me all your money yet, now would be a good time to do so.

letters OF support

Dear T.O. Strong,

Thank you very much for your book. I never knew just how much you would help me out. I used to waste all my time caring. I'd volunteer at the food bank, help the elderly, and visit children in the hospital burn unit. I once spent two years in Africa digging irrigation ditches in the hot sun to help the needy farmers there. What a waste of time!

Your book has taught me the selfishness I have always lacked. No longer will I let the sick and needy run my life. Now it's time to look out for No. 1! I have even started a petition in my neighbourhood to get rid of a group home. You wouldn't believe how slow and aggravating these people are! And to think, just a year ago I would probably have volunteered there. What a fool I was.

Blissfully yours,
Lorain McTire

Mr. Strong,

Thank you for your enlightening book. I am pleased with the results. Not only am I more small-minded and intolerant than before, but I have also lost all of my friends. I have no idea where they went. My wife would know, but she left me before I even got to Step Three. I am very happy she left. No longer will I have to endure her endless chatter and babble. She just didn't know when to shut up and would go on and on and on. Sometimes I thought she'd never stop, but now I don't have to listen to her anymore. I bet she's making small talk somewhere right now. "Oh, do you think it will rain tomorrow?" she'd be saying to some shop attendant. "No, it looks like it is going to clear up," the shop attendant might respond. "Oh, I hope you're right," she'd say next, and then she'd run her hand through her silky black hair and flash that smile of hers. Oh, that smile. And those ruby red lips. Oh, how I miss her. Why did she leave me? Why did I ever read your book? She's gone! GONE! And now I have nothing. My socks don't even match anymore. I swear, no two are the same. My socks were perfect when she was here, but now I have uncoordinated feet. One red and one brown. How did this happen? I don't even own a red sock. Oh darling, if you read this, please come back. I miss you so much. Every day is like a trip to hell for me. Ohhhhhhhhhhhhhhhhhhhhhh! My heart is throwing itself against my chest, hoping to break free so it can run off and be with you once again. Oh how my body yearns to be near you. At night, I dream you have returned and are organizing my sock drawer.

Keep up the good work,

Lester Beebof

To TO

This iz a lettur to thenk yu so much fer all yer
help. I uzed to be mad when peepel made fun of me
cuz I wuz so stoopid. now I no that tha r the
ones who shuld be mad cuz I am ok. Som still laf
at me but I punch em in the hed an then thei shut
up. They bleed lots and mak my underwar mesy so I
half to wash it.

Yu reel gud,
Gus

Thank you, Mr. Strong!

Because of you I have been able to realize all of my dreams. My entire life, I've been a loser and a drifter. I'd wander from place to place and always end up worse off than before. That's behind me now. Because of your book I live the kind of life I never would have dreamed of. I live in a very large building with attendants catering to my every need. A team of chefs cooks my meals, I no longer have to work, and I exercise frequently in a large yard. And my social life has become more intense, with violent, passionate engagements — often in the shower! So, cheers to you! Dreams do come true.

Herbert Brookner
Cell 4309, Devil's Knee Correctional Facility

Hi T.O.!

I just want to thank you for your wonderful book. I've been
reading self-help books for years now, and yours is
absolutely the best. I've actually burned all the others.
Isn't that great?

Well, my husband was the one who gave me your book for
Christmas because he saw that it said it was "the last self-
help book you will ever read," and, well, I've read a lot.
He'd try anything to get me to stop. At the time I was taking
yoga, and eating an all-mango diet. I grew the mangoes
myself to ensure their freshness, which is very expensive to
do in Winnipeg. I also had my own personal guru named Swami
Sven. He was very expensive, and put me through exercises
which I thought were helpful at the time, but now I'm not so
sure. Most of them involved me sitting on his lap. I also
used to go to a psychic who helped me explore my past lives.
I discovered that I was Lincoln and John Wilkes Booth at the
same time, and the reason that Booth shot Lincoln was that I
was spreading myself too thin. I was also the Policeman in
the Village People. But now I'm pretty sure this didn't
happen. It was all so confusing, especially since Swami Sven
believed in reincarnation, and said that I was going to come
back as a desk at IKEA, and that's why all IKEA furniture
has cute little names.

But now I'm free of all this clutter. Now I believe only
in you. I will never be brainwashed again. I will never be
brainwashed again. I will never be brainwashed again. I will
never be brainwashed again.

My husband's gone now, as are the kids, and I live in
our old Hugo car, just me and my troll dolls. I like the
ones with purple hair best. In fact, I don't think it's fair
that trolls can grow hair in all those fascinating colours
while people can't do that at all. I don't know why that is.
Maybe you should have a chapter on troll dolls in your next
book. I'd buy it for sure!

Thanks. You are a great, great, man.

Margaret Hoofdernoof

Dear Dad,

I'm hungry. Mommy said if I wrote you, then you might send money. Mommy's not feeling good. She is sick almost every day. I tell her not to smoke so much, but she says she needs to smoke at the craps table or she will lose her edge. I'm helping Mommy out by working at my own job. I go from casino to casino taking tokens from people who are too drunk to pay attention to me. I am very good. I have only been caught twice, and like Mommy says, they can't lock me up because I am so small. Mommy just coughed again. It's the same sound I remember the car making the morning you left. Please send money so I can eat and Mommy can smoke.

Love,
Clarence

P.S. — I've had many new daddies since you, but you are still one of the better ones.

Glossary

ALL WORDS HAVE ONE MEANING

There are many words in this book. For this, I am truly sorry, but don't worry — I've provided this glossary to help you out. If there's a word in this book that you need to understand, just look it up here. Do not use a dictionary! They cannot be trusted.

AC/DC — The only band worth listening to.

Alcohol — A miracle chemical that makes you think less clearly.

Alienation — A positive sign that you have progressed past other people.

Ambition — An infection of motivation. Often fatal.

Amsterdam — A large city frequented by young North Americans seeking prostitutes, drugs, and wooden shoes.

Andes — A bunch of mountains out in some country somewhere. They are supposed to be very tall and snowy. People afflicted with ambition often try to climb mountains "because they are there." What's wrong with a couch? It's there too.

Animals — Creatures that exist for your personal enjoyment. Animals can be eaten, skinned, or run over in your car.

Art — An object of no value that someone wants you to buy.

Artist — Someone who wants you to buy his art.

Astronauts – People who claim to have been in space. They are lying. The whole space program was a just a big advertising campaign to sell Tang.

Awareness — A dangerous condition where you notice what is happening around you.

Baby — A tiny monster whose size belies its terrible destructive powers.

Black-toed three-legged weed-hopper — A curious animal that now exists only on a single patch of grass on a traffic island in Luxembourg. Weed-hoppers are born with four legs, but after a painful childbirth, the mother eats one out of spite.

Blame — Something you give and never receive.

Bliss — The perfect state of being — obtained when you know nothing and feel even less.

Blumpt the Cosmic Slug — A 15-million-mile-long slug that slithered across the universe leaving a trail of slime that later became parking enforcement officials. Blumpt becomes angry and vengeful when she is not invited to parties.

Box 48, Grim Canyon, Nevada — The address to send your money to.

Brain — An organ, like the appendix, with no known purpose. It is best to have it removed as early as possible.

British Monarchy — An inbred clan who give newspapers something to write about on slow days.

Broccoli — A green vegetable with ugly hair. Mothers often force children to eat it. It contains no nutrients, only evil.

Cars — Motorized conveyances used to run over animals, into telephone poles, and through therapists.

Cavalcade of Superheroes — An organization of superpowered beings. Current membership includes: the Cosmic Chicken, Captain Apathy, and the Human Fungus.

Cavemen — A primitive, unthinking people who knew almost nothing about anything. Where did we go wrong?

Challenges — Struggles that must be ignored.

Charcoal Drawing — An art designed to degrade and belittle students in school. Only losers make charcoal drawings.

Cheesies — The food of life.

Cheez Whiz — A good source of orange food dye. The name is slightly misleading: it contains no cheez, only whiz.

Child Support — A ridiculous law forcing one parent to give money to the other just because they foolishly kept the child.

Children — Older babies. Children cannot be easily disposed of, but may have "accidents."

Christmas — A "holiday" created by greeting-card companies to rob the world.

Cigarettes — Healthy tobacco tubes that make you look cool.

Closure — A term created by therapists to give the illusion that one day your problem will be solved. There is not a single recorded case of a therapist achieving closure without first "discovering" another problem.

Conspiracy — The fact that everyone is out to get you.

Crapatania — A small Third World nation whose main exports are dysentery and depression.

Crazy — Something others will call you because they fear the truth.

Credit Cards — Free money.

DDT — A miracle chemical that kills animals, and mutates their offspring in amusing ways.

Death — The end of life. This does not apply to you.

Debt — A fountain of free money.

Denial — The perfect state of being, when your reality becomes the only reality.

Dentist — A horrible person who places a small vacuum in your mouth and then engages you in conversation. Dentists also place fillings in your mouth containing radio transmitters to monitor you.

Disney — The company that patented a method of maximizing trite emotions.

DNA — Doopy Noopy Aboo.

Donahue — Oprah's dark herald.

Dr. Phil — Oprah's lieutenant. He paid his dues as Barney the Dinosaur.

Doonesbury — A cartoon so clever nobody laughs.

Drugs — Perfectly safe, non-addictive personality enhancers.

Easter — A holiday created by chocolate-egg manufacturers (who are more powerful than one might suppose).

Elvis — The great singer who faked his own death so he could drink booze, pop pills, and get fat, in private.

Emperor — What you become when you achieve total ignorance.

Entertainment Tonight — The only truthful newscast.

Exercise — Ridiculous, repetitive movements that waste vital life force.

Ex-wives — Harpies that hound you to the ends of the earth. Just leave me alone! You're not getting one red cent. I'll move to Cuba if I have to, or fake my own death. You'll never bleed me dry!

Family — Something you inherit at birth and spend a whole life trying to lose.

Father — A man who leaves you at a young age.

Feelings — Artificial constructs that impede the functioning of day-to-day life.

Food — Dead things you put in your mouth.

Freedom — What you gain at the expense of others.

Friends — People who use you for their own selfish needs.

Gladiators — The ancient practitioners of professional wrestling.

Glossary — What you are reading now.

Goal — An object of effort that you will never achieve and will probably die trying for. Your only goal should be to have no goal, and you shouldn't even achieve that.

God — An old guy with a really long beard who sits up in heaven and has better things to do than to listen to you complain.

Government — The bastards who take your money and occasionally throw you in jail.

Greeks — An ancient people who liked olives.

Greeting Cards — Nefarious devices more dangerous than therapy and education combined. Each contains a mind-controlling message that worms into your brain. They are usually introduced in kindergarten on Valentine's Day. All the other kids got lots of them, but I never got any… but I'm glad I didn't, because look at those kids now! They are all victims of love, while I am free! Free! I hate them.

Guilt — A feeling invented by the Catholic Church that can only be relieved by giving them money.

Guns — Man's best friend.

Healing Circle — A geometric whining contest where the winner is the one who cries the most.

Hippies — Grubby, smelly, sixties throwbacks who pretend to care about "issues" but really just want to smoke up, wear ugly clothes, and complain about "the man."

Ignorance — The ability to care enough not to care and know enough not to know.

Inadequacy — A feeling others experience when they try to measure up to you.

Industrial Revolution — A time when cows, goats, and horses went on strike, forcing people to create machines as scab labour.

Inner Voice — A tiny voice inside your head that tells you to do things. This voice comes from fillings in your teeth.

Jerry Springer — A wonderful man who hosts a TV show that explores the real issues of today.

Kennedy Family — Famous American political family that liked to drink and screw around. Often shot.

King of Glastenshite — The ruler of a magical land where thought has not been invented, emotions do not exist, and fountains flow with liquid meat.

Koalas — Weird animals that eat only one type of plant and complain if they don't get it.

Laws — Rules others make and you ignore.

Liberace — A glittering collection of costumes that played piano.

Liberal Arts — A university program preparing students for a life of unobtainable dreams.

Lottery Ticket — A surefire path to riches.

Louvre — A large building in Frenchland with lots of stupid pictures.

Love — An emotion that creates weakness, dependency, and dementia.

Lunar Landing — An event that never happened. It was a film made in a studio. They did this to create the saying "They can put a man on the moon." This was to encourage people to think anything was possible. As you know, nothing is possible.

Marriage — Good grounds for divorce.

Martha Stewart — A fiendish humanoid robot created by the therapists to induce stress and striving in normal people's lives.

Menhir — A very large rock that ancient people rolled around before the discovery of bowling.

Microsoft — An accumulation of geeks and nerds that create products they would never use.

Middle Class — People who work in cubicles for forty years so they can save enough money to buy the world's most advanced wheelchair when they retire.

Missy Macmillan — A girl who didn't know what she could have had. Why didn't you ever give me a valentine? Why? I hate you… I didn't mean that. Or did I?

Modern Dance — Dance so advanced it has no dancing.

Money — The basic building block of self-worth.

Monkeys — Funny little proto-humans that eat bananas and look adorable in hats. Good to conduct experiments on.

Morondavia — An Eastern European nation that manufactures wet-naps.

Mother — A nagging presence that refuses to let you forget where you came from.

Motorcycle — Noisy, powered bicycles that show everyone how ignorant you are.

Mr. Ed — A horse that could talk. Although highly realistic, he was just an illusion, like the lunar landings.

Mr. Morgan — I'll get you, Mr. Morgan!

Mu-Mu the Monkeyhead — A large god with a monkey's head and a fish's body that breathes snails and has laser-beam eyes that it uses to etch its name into park benches.

Munsters (The) — A bunch of monsters that lived together and did funny things. Unlike the lunar landings and Mr. Ed, they were real.

Nature — A term created by hippies for anything they like. Avoid nature.

Oedipal Complex — The Freudian theory that every boy wants to kill his dad, sleep with his mom, and play poker with his dogs.

Opinions — A stance on any given topic. Only yours matter. Why other people have opinions is still unknown.

Oprah — The face of the self-help cartel. It is not known if she is the real power or merely a figurehead. It is rumoured that Donald Duck actually calls the shots.

Original Sin — A guilt cover charge.

Pandas — Big stupid animals that eat only Chinese food.

Pants — A useless piece of clothing that makes it harder to put on your underwear.

Peace — A sense of calm experienced when you destroy your enemies.

Penguins — The Dark Overlords of Antarctica.

Philosophy — The art of sounding smart while being dumb.

Pills — Solutions in a bottle.

Pit Bull — Your furry friend who uses neighbours as chew toys.

Pizza — The fruit of the pizza tree.

Pizza Guy — The only human you should still be in regular contact with.

Police — Thugs hired by the therapists to push you around.

Pop-Tarts — The most advanced food on earth. Made entirely of plastics and perfectly rectangular, Pop-Tarts contain filling with colours not found in nature. A balanced diet consists of Pop-Tarts, booze, and cigarettes.

Psychologist — A high priest of the conspiracy who invents new feelings and disorders to inflict on the world.

Pyramids — Large buildings based on some sort of geometric form, but I'm not sure exactly what that is.

Religion — A collection of beliefs people follow to complicate their lives.

Sandwich — The most complex food you should ever eat.

School — A building infested with teachers.

Self-help Book — A book designed leave you a jelly-filled, doubting mess.

Sesame Street — Part of the conspiracy to infect children with feelings; featuring furry space aliens. And just where was this street anyway? Was it part of the lunar landing set? Did they drink Tang? Was Mr. Morgan there with his charcoal drawings? You draw your own conclusions. No, actually, I'll draw them for you.

Sigmund Freud — An Austrian bearing very little resemblance to Arnold Schwarzenegger except that he probably also had a funny accent. Sigmund created therapy so he'd have money to buy smokes. Unfortunately, things got out of hand.

Slaves — What you were before you read my book. I have released you from the conspiracy. Now you are free to do what I tell you.

Soul — A mystical entity that represents your intangible spirit. Worth selling to the highest bidder.

Spam — Tasty congealed meat stuff. Also useful as a body rub.

Squirrels — A surprisingly tasty snack.

Star Trek — A glimpse into the future, where everyone speaks English and dresses in pajamas.

Star Wars — The film they made after the lunar landing hoax. People wouldn't believe it, so they sold it as a movie.

Stonehenge — A bunch of big rocks in a circle. It was used as a ring in prehistoric professional wrestling matches.

Stress — Unnecessary anxiety caused by challenges. Easily cured by apathy.

Teenager — What a child becomes when you feed it too much. They get bigger than you, crash your car, and burn down your house. If you have children, it is best to keep them in a little box. That way they'll stay smaller than you.

Therapist — A person who takes your money and makes you feel bad.

Therapy — The art of opening mental wounds and keeping them that way.

Thinking — The act of creating thoughts. Never, ever do this.

Three's Company — A wonderful show that explored the zany mis-understandings of three roommates — two women and one man. The man's name was Jack Tripper and his landlord thought he was gay. Often a couple of characters would have a conversation in one room and the character in the other room would misinterpret it as something sexual — although there was never any real sex, gay or otherwise, on the series. Even the Ropers couldn't get laid, and they were married.

Tibet — A useless, cold, mountainous country mired in poverty. It is so miserable that it is often assumed that the inhabitants must contain some special spiritual strength just to get through the day. The truth is they simply don't have a choice.

T.O. Strong — The great man who saved your life. You owe everything to him. If you had money, you would send it to him. If he were in jail, you would sacrifice your own life to set him free.

Tobacco Multinationals — Good wholesome companies looking out for the good of mankind.

Truth — The words in this book.

Umbilical Cord — A piece of tubing attached to your bellybutton at birth. Good in soups.

Underwear — The perfect outfit.

Vegemite — An Australian yeast spread that goes well with nothing.

Walls — Barriers that keep the annoying world at bay.

Whales — Self-important animals who the hippies are always trying to save. If you weigh ten tons you should be able to handle your own problems. Don't come bugging me.

Wife — Something I have never had — several times.

Ignorance Quotient Test Results

MARKING SCHEME

First, find the values of your six different ICs (Ignorance Clumps) by adding up the results in the following manner:

IC #1
For questions 3, 8, 12, 22, and 23.
A = 1 pt
B = 3 pt
C = 5 pt
D = 7 pt
IC #1 = _____

IC #2
For questions 1, 13, 15, 16, and 17.
A = 5 pt
B = -2 pt
C = 2 pt
D = 3
IC #2 = _____

IC #3
For question 5.
A = 2
B = 2
C = 2
D = 2
IC #3 = _____

IC #4
For questions 2, 6, 7, 18, 19, 20, 24, and 25.
A = 0
B = 12
C = 34
D = 2
C #4 = _____

IC #5
For questions 4, 9,10,11, and 14.

A = B

B = 3

C = B + A - B

D = N/A

IC #5 = _____

IC #6
For question 23 and any others I might have missed.

A = .3

B = 23

C = 78

D = 657

IC #6 = _____

To Calculate Your Score

Multiply IC #1 by IC #2. Divide this by the square root of IC #3. Subtract the numerical equivalent of the alphabetical placing of all the letters in your mother's maiden name (if her name is hyphenated, assign the hyphen the value of 5). Add the value of IC #4. Subtract your height in cubits. Multiply by IC #5 and forget all about IC #6. Divide the result you have by its own value. Find a black cat and bury it in your backyard on the darkest day of the year. Now put your right foot in, now take your right foot out, now put your right foot in and shake it all about.

Turn to the next page to analyze your result.

You have failed!

The stupid do not check.